Palgrave Texts in Counselling and Psychotherapy

Series Editors
Arlene Vetere
Family Therapy and Systemic Practice
VID Specialized University
Oslo, UK

Rudi Dallos
Clinical Psychology
Plymouth University
Plymouth, UK

This series introduces readers to the theory and practice of counselling and psychotherapy across a wide range of topical issues. Ideal for both trainees and practitioners, the books will appeal to anyone wishing to use counselling and psychotherapeutic skills and will be particularly relevant to workers in health, education, social work and related settings. The books in this series emphasise an integrative orientation weaving together a variety of models including, psychodynamic, attachment, trauma, narrative and systemic ideas. The books are written in an accessible and readable style with a focus on practice. Each text offers theoretical background and guidance for practice, with creative use of clinical examples.

Jim Wilson

Building Creative Therapeutic Relationships with Children and Young People

The Playfully Serious Practitioner

palgrave
macmillan

Jim Wilson
Newport, Gwent, UK

ISSN 2662-9127 ISSN 2662-9135 (electronic)
Palgrave Texts in Counselling and Psychotherapy
ISBN 978-3-031-85705-8 ISBN 978-3-031-85706-5 (eBook)
https://doi.org/10.1007/978-3-031-85706-5

Cover illustration: Raul Garcia Herrera / Alamy Stock Photo

This Palgrave Macmillan imprint is published by the registered company Springer Nature Switzerland AG.
The registered company address is: Gewerbestrasse 11, 6330 Cham, Switzerland

Dedication

To my mentors, teachers and clients that have helped me to develop as a family therapist since 1978. Thank you also to the following: The Scottish Institute of Human Relations, Edinburgh, for the initial spark of inspiration, colleagues at Carnegie Clinic, Dunfermline, for their open-hearted support in the early days, the Sick Children's Hospital in Edinburgh and Les Scarth in particular, for noticing my potential, Somerset Social Services for their encouragement in bringing family therapy into their service, The Family Institute Cardiff for providing me with the unique opportunity to spread my wings as a trainer, therapist and author, Barry Mason and The Institute of Family Therapy, London, for providing freedom to develop the Centre for Child Studies, the dedicated and inspiring colleagues of Greenwich Child and Adolescent Mental Health Service (CAMHS) at Shooters Hill, the staff of Llwyn Onn Child and Family Psychology Service in Caerleon for their enthusiastic support of my practice over the years, my online friends and colleagues in the Politics In Practice group with special thanks to Peter Jakob, and my fellow members of the Open Dialogical Practices group, Justine van Lawick, Jaakko Seikkula, John Shotter and Peter Rober for helping to keep creativity alive in my practice.

Gianfranco Cecchin of the Milan Associates and Tom Andersen require a special mention as I have kept their influence alive in my mind and in my heart throughout my practice. They inspire me still.

Acknowledgements

Thank you to the series editors and for Arlene Vetere's unstinting support in helping the book come to life. Thank you to Sian my wife for helping me to make the time to get on with it!

Contents

1

Introduction: Inspiration and Brevity

> I am still a child. I am learning. My name, Satyarthi means, 'student of truth,' and I want to remain like that. If I remain a child, I remain a student.

The words of Kailash Satyarthi, joint winner, with Malala Yousafzai, of the Nobel Peace Prize 2014 for their struggle against the suppression of all children and young people and the right of all children to education.

Being invited to write this practice-based book made me concentrate on the core ideas and practices that I have found useful in my development as a systemic (family) therapist over forty years. My hope is that this book will stimulate your creativity in your practice and inspire new opportunities when you meet with children and young people. At the same time as adding to your skills, it is important to never underestimate those well-honed abilities already in your repertoire that help you to conduct the jobs you do with a sense of competence, focus and satisfaction.

What is vitally important is our capacity to review, correct, challenge, and enhance our practice repertoires especially where we have become "stuck in a rut" or lacking in fresh enthusiasm or curiosity. Miller and Hubble (2011) propose that our development requires "consistently and consciously pushing to reach objectives just beyond one's level of

J. Wilson, *Building Creative Therapeutic Relationships with Children and Young People*,
Palgrave Texts in Counselling and Psychotherapy,
https://doi.org/10.1007/978-3-031-85706-5_1

proficiency" (p. 25). There is a circular process between our actions and the ways we think. Ideas can inform and shape our actions and our actions, in turn, may inform our ideas. An important skill for any therapist is their capacity to critically reflect on ideas and reappraise actions, especially when actions and ideas lead us nowhere with our clients.[1] As Satyarthi suggests, we are all students and if we remain open minded, we will continue to expand our capabilities as practitioners.[2]

Meeting children and young people in distress is not a technical application of protocols and procedures. It is a human encounter, a multi-sensorial exchange within which different practice methods and techniques have a place, and these will be explored in the following chapters. Their place is situated within the unique relational context between practitioner, child and those important others in the child's life. Professional practice is further influenced by one's professional context and workplace. Where services for children are under immense pressure or where managerial protocols restrict opportunities to put in place appropriate services for our clients, the therapist/practitioner can feel overwhelmed and unable to fully demonstrate their creativity. It is therefore crucial to consider such constraints and find creative options to address limitations that interrupt or restrict effective practice (Wilson, 2017). These features of the practitioner's working context will also be explored in the forthcoming pages. We are, primarily, social beings and our focus needs to pay serious attention to the various contexts of a child's life that help to shape who s/he[3] is and how one can best try to help.

[1] I have opted for the term "'client"' as a generic description of those children and young people who are receiving a professional service. Alternative descriptions may be inserted by the reader such as "'patient"' or "'service user" 'whilst acknowledging that each definition places a different emphasis on the construction of the relationship between the practitioner and the children he /she meets.

[2] I will use the generic term "practitioner" and "therapist" "interchangeably to encompass all those professionals working in social and mental health services with children and their families. When I talk of my own practice, I specifically use the term "therapist" to denote my designation as a systemic family therapist.

[3] I will vary the gender of the practitioner to avoid overuse of she/he/they. Where children's circumstances are described in case studies, I will use their given gender identity, though for reasons of confidentiality some details of their situation may be altered.

Co-Creativity and Playfully Serious Practice

Creativity is considered in this context as: "The ability to produce work that is both novel (original, unexpected) and appropriate, useful, adaptive, concerning task constraints" (Sternberg, 2010, p. 3). It is also important to see creativity as a way of recombining already present, though perhaps not visible, means to more creative possibilities. Arthur Koestler (1964) defines the creative process "…not (as) an act of creation in the sense of the Old Testament. It does not create something out of nothing; it uncovers, selects, re-shuffles, combines, synthesizes, already existing facts, ideas, faculties, skills. The more familiar the parts the more striking the new whole" (p. 120)

Co-creativity focuses attention on the relational aspects of creative possibilities between all participants. It is not the sole preserve of the therapist; rather the therapist's task is to try to create the conditions, with others, where fresh initiatives, responses, and ideas emerge in dialogue. Co-creative dialogue in therapy requires the capacity of the therapist and others to depart from the status quo of praxis, to improvise and challenge "domesticated" practices and ideas that inhibit change. A search for psychosocial resources, apparent or latent within the therapeutic context, is a central focus in this approach (see Wilson, 2021).

The Vygotskian definition of play and his concept of a zone of proximal development capture the relational, contextual, features of play and its developmental character. "In play a child is always above his average age, above his daily behaviour; in play it is as though he were a head taller than himself … play contains all developmental tendencies in a condensed form; in play it is as though the child were trying to jump above the level of his normal behaviour" (Vygotski, 1967, p. 16).

The book has a dual purpose: it aims to provide readers with an orientation to practice that illustrates the learning and growth that occurs in children and their families in therapy, ***and also*** how a playfully serious orientation can enrich the skill set and repertoire of the therapist/practitioner.

Co-creativity in practice emerges in a context of exploration between participants. To take practice seriously , to deal with the tragedies of life, one also benefits from tapping into the playfulness in our encounters with others .This is not to minimise the seriousness of practice; rather, it is to allow oneself to see the importance of playing with ideas , playing with techniques , stretching the imagination, finding fresh means to usefully connect with our clients and entertaining a degree of irreverence and challenge towards those practices that would objectify our clients. Playfully serious practice and rigorous thinking are not mutually exclusive categories. The famous comic actor and filmmaker Charlie Chaplin, when asked about the rigour demanded in making a film, mentions the importance of the accumulation of his learning over time that allowed him a degree of spontaneity in filmmaking. He remarked, "…all creative work is done out of excitement and enthusiasm. … we start that way." How to remain enthusiastic about practice is an important question since finding satisfaction and inspiration infuses practice, and transfers into meetings with the children and young people we meet. It is worth noting that the people we meet in our practice judge whether a therapist is fully present with them or is simply going through a tired routine. How we begin really matters.

References

Cole, E., John-Steiner,V., Scribner, S., & Souberman, E. (Eds). (1978). L. S. Vygotsky: Mind In Society; Development of Higher Psychological Processes. Cambridge: Harvard University Press.

Koestler, A. (1964). *The act of creation*. Arkana.

Miller, S., & Hubble, M. (2011). The road to mastery. *Psychotherapy Networker, 35*(3), 22–31, 60.

Sternberg, R. J. (Ed.). (2010). *Handbook of creativity*. Cambridge University Press.

Wilson, J. (2017). *Creativity in times of constraint: A practitioner's companion in mental health and social care*. Routledge.

Wilson, J. (2021). Boxed in?: Commentary on widening the screen: Playful responses to challenges in online therapy with children and families. *Journal of Family Therapy, 43*(2), 346–350.

2

Playfully Serious Practice: Parameters and Perspectives

We Are, Firstly, Social, Relational Beings

In June 2021 Arthur Labinjo-Hughes, aged six, was murdered by his father's partner. His brain damage was consistent with being struck against a wall. His small body was skeletal and video footage of his last days showed him so weakened that he could not lift a duvet from the floor. The video also caught him saying to himself, "Nobody loves me." The detailed accounts of the trial of his father and partner made dismaying but all too familiar reading of systemic failure between agencies with a duty of care for children.

To meet with a child in therapy is not simply to **see** them or to **hear** their words. It is a matter of meeting the child as a whole person who is embedded in his unique relational context.

Apparently when an investigating social worker visited the parent's home following an allegation that Arthur was being abused, the social worker asked the question of Arthur, "On a scale of nought to ten how happy are you?" The child replied, "Ten." Only later in court does it become evident that the child was under threat from his father to provide this "happy" response for fear of being taken away from home. Arthur's

J. Wilson, *Building Creative Therapeutic Relationships with Children and Young People*, Palgrave Texts in Counselling and Psychotherapy,
https://doi.org/10.1007/978-3-031-85706-5_2

words were taken as a true reflection of his feelings instead of reading "between the lines" and noticing the finer details of the child's forced "happy "reply. What was missing was an appreciation of the context of fear and intimidation, in which Arthur's life was ordered. Apparently, the false reassurance from Arthur's father to the social worker that the boy's bruises were the result of "boisterous play" was accepted unchallenged. Had the social worker been able to explore the detail of the boisterous play, it could have led to a more precise assessment and realisation that boisterous play does not result in bruises on the scale and seriousness suffered by Arthur. A more perceptive, investigative interview with the parent was needed but not pursued. But the most striking feature of the reports on Arthur was the failure by professionals to engage directly with Arthur without the intimidating presence of his father.

We are, first, social, relational beings and every sense needs to be brought to bear on our attempts to meet and connect with children. However, if practitioners are fearful, anxious, lacking support, and reactive rather than reflective, we can miss what later seems so obvious, as with young Arthur. Anxiety can make us search for certainty, eliminate complexity and smother curiosity. We lose sight of wider contextual influences on our practice and fail to comprehend the full picture of a child's life.

Donald Winnicott, psychoanalyst and child psychotherapist, described his practice with children as "...always a meeting point between us as participants, not between us as an experiment. ... The subject for study is intercommunication between me and the patient. ... meeting on equal terms each teaching the other and getting enriched by the experience of involvement. ... This is the same as form in art ... which allows for a spontaneous impulse and the unexpected creative gesture. This is what we wait for and value highly in our work and we even hold back on our bright ideas when they come for fear of blocking the bright ideas that might come from the child or adult patient" (Winnicott in Shepherd et al., 1996, p. 278).

A systemic approach (Hoffman, 2002; Dallos & Draper, 2010; Wilson, 2003) emphasises the child's experience as both an expression of her as a person in her own right and a member of her family and the multiple contexts that help to shape her sense of her identity, that is, to work systemically with a child is to work with the ***child-in-context.***

Clearly with Arthur the context was nowhere safe enough to play in the Winnicottian sense. To make practice safe enough to play, a systemic approach takes Winnicott's definition and widens it into a broader relational context of the child's life. In systemic terms the meeting point includes engagement with the child, the child's family and other significant people in his life. If this is not possible or practical, then at the very least the practitioner holds this relational context at the forefront of her thinking.

To meet *WITH* a child in therapy means finding connections that imaginatively try to connect with their experience and tap into their psychosocial resources. To do this the practitioner has to find a way to attune not only to the child but to the surrounding contexts of his life. Children meet us in their words and actions, and we are more likely to connect with them when we notice how the child's words are spoken and how their feelings and impressions touch us emotionally. To explore ways to work creatively with children is a challenge that asks of us to extend our practice without losing touch with the wider contexts that can profoundly influence what we see and, as in the case of young Arthur, what we can miss.

Systemic Change: Introducing a Not Too Unusual Difference

Change, from a systemic perspective, is geared towards opening up possibilities that help the child and others in his life to move away from repetitive patterns of thinking, action and experiences that restrict their creative power to deal with problems in life.

Aside: I recall an introductory session with Bill, a fifteen-year-old boy, and his parents in which I was trying too hard to create a conversation with Bill. The more I enquired after his opinions (his views on coming to therapy, his wishes for a positive outcome) the more he slumped back into his chair and mumbled, "I don't know". At last, his father said, "Bill told me before he came here that he wasn't going to talk!"

This gave me a moment to reconsider my previous attempts to engage Bill. I said to him (something like) "Bill, please do not talk. It is important that you should not talk if you don't wish to. In my experience young people decide when they are willing to join in a conversation. So please don't join in unless or until you'd like to do so. Instead, I will talk with your parents right now and, from time to time, I may ask your views on what they have to say but please don't feel obliged to join in the conversation."

Bill looked a little bemused by my instruction which seemed to contradict his expectation that he would be obliged to talk to a therapist.

Reflection on this sequence:

I was failing to engage Bill in conversation and his father helped by telling me about Bill's prior decision not to talk to me. Moreover, his father provided me with a much-needed moment of reflection that allowed me to fully appreciate the redundant pattern of interaction with Bill and prompted me to ***do something different***. I decided to accept Bill's position of "refusing to talk" and, instead I invited him to be an observer of the conversation I would have with his parents. I also guessed that Bill would not be able to keep silent when he listened to his parents' complaints, as I reckoned he was quite a central figure in the family and liked to make his views heard.

This is an illustration of the practitioner noticing a redundant pattern and deciding to change direction. It happens regularly in practice and is only a problem when practitioners fail to notice when such patterns are unproductive. In short, as practitioners we need to alter our responses to the responses from our clients when the pattern becomes unproductive. The worst error is failing to observe ourselves and our reactions, and instead blaming the client for being "unmotivated and resistant." This objectifies the child or young person and assumes the fault in making a useful connection lies solely with them. In this instance Bill liked the idea of being an observer and before too long he was quite keen to offer his opinions! It was a beginning….

The therapist John Weakland, co-founder of the Brief Therapy Center in Palo Alto, California (Fisch et al., 1982), once described the difference between ***difficulties*** in life and ***problems*** in life as follows (I have paraphrased): "Difficulties are just one thing after another. … Problems are the same damn thing time and time again!" (personal communication). At a certain point in life, we find solutions to problems of living that at a later point may no longer apply. This is encapsulated in the expression "The solution has become the problem." The therapist's job is to find options to alter such confining patterns, and seek out psychosocial resources in the child's life. This involves those significant others in her life wherever possible. However, it is also important to appreciate the rationale offered by family members on "how things have come to be the way they are." That is, each person's explanations and ideas about causation of the problems they are experiencing. First, the aim is to try to appreciate the logic of another person's views and, second, to be curious about how these views sustain the current family interaction. This stops me from jumping to conclusions and helps me to look for openings in the interaction that might provide new, more useful directions.

In order to promote a change towards more useful directions to help a child, the therapist must gauge the degree of support and challenge he can try to promote. If he challenges a family member's viewpoint without firstly conveying a sense of respect and appreciation of the person, his challenges are likely to be resisted. Instead of "head on" challenges that will go nowhere, the therapist looks to see where a connection can be made that will be accepted as a possible new route in the conversation.

A very truculent and angry father came with his fourteen-year-old son to a family session at my clinic and stated, almost before we had sat down, "I don't give a fuck about you … [pointing at me] … I don't give a fuck about you either … [pointing to my colleague]. … I give a fuck about him … [pointing to his now very embarrassed son].

To my ears his angry words did not carry threat, but feelings of desperation, and the manner of the father's delivery also struck me as oddly comical. I smiled inside. I was moved more by his way of expressing his concern and care for his son than bothered about his Anglo-Saxon expletives. His anger was an expression of his desire to get help for his depressed son. I said, "*I agree. That is the main thing! To get help for your son. That is what we will try to do.*" The father seemed to settle more into his chair. What mattered here was the tone of the father's words. They carried a desperation that conveyed to me that he was not so dismissive of my colleague and me, more that he was very anxious to get help. Attending to the tone of his words allowed a more engaging response from us.

Had I reacted in an indignant manner by saying, for example, "*There is no need to use foul language towards us. We are here to help!*" I think the father would have felt chastised and his unspoken message, "*Please help my son,*" would not have been heard or responded. We gauge how to introduce a difference into the opening conversation with the clients we meet, and while protocols for conducting family sessions are useful (see Chap. 3) we are nonetheless improvising responses to the often-unexpected words and actions of our clients.

What Is Meant by the Term Playfully Serious Practice?

The tragic death of young Arthur Labinjo-Hughes emphasises the seriousness of providing a therapeutic, child-focused service to children and young people that attends to ethical matters concerned with the protection of children from harm. All therapeutic practice is a process of humanisation for all participants, not a technological application of protocols (Freire, 1996, 1998; Wilson, 2013). Theories about therapy and child development and the plethora of practice techniques and methodologies may all play a useful part in the therapist's skill set. But dogged loyalty to certainty about the "right" theory, the "right" approach and the "right" intervention can lead to problems of professional hubris and stop therapists from critically appraising their own prejudices about what they see and do in their practice. This is where a playfully serious attitude challenges such hubris and single-minded certainties. The practitioner needs both the capacity to respect ideas, theories and the accumulation of knowledge and, at the same time, remain open to innovation and improvisation.

Play and Improvisation

We improvise all the time (Santi, 2010) and our capacity to improvise when we meet with our clients is crucial. It is the difference between being able to read a score of music (the equivalent of our laid down protocols and methods) and picking up an instrument to play music spontaneously (what we do with the methods we have studied).

Christopher Heimann (2009), teacher of improvisation at the Royal Academy of Dramatic Art, describes the following abilities required of an improvisational actor . I believe that the skills he outlines here have a certain resonance with skills that enhance the playfully serious practitioner's orientation to practice. Heimann argues that development in improvisation requires us to undo some of our normal educational processes and recapture some of our childlike abilities. He includes these abilities: "to be fully absorbed in what we are doing, to be curious, vulnerable and open, truly affected by the people and things we interact with, to be present in sensorial experience and an ability to act spontaneously and intuitively, to experience without judgement, and the ability to surprise ourselves and others." He sums up these abilities as our capacity to play (in Wilson, 2017).

Playfulness is a serious ingredient in the therapist's attitude to his development. To play with ideas is **to allow oneself to avoid dogma in any application of a method of therapy**. We challenge ourselves to place our certainties, our prejudices, in parentheses (after Cecchin et al., 1994) and allow alternative ideas to be entertained. This process helps to stem the hubris of expert-driven ideas from taking root. It does not mean we lack expertise but rather expertise is considered a craft that is always open to fresh initiative, fresh opportunities to keep creativity alive in our work. Therapeutic conversation is a[1] generative process (Gergen, 2009) that, handled sensitively in child-focused practice, can lead to changes in perspectives and responses from others in the child's life as well as in the child's own experience.

[1] Generating forms of dialogue that attempt to," "locate fissures in the taken for granted realities of the disputants ... that enable participants to generate a new and more promising domain of shared meaning ... the chief emphasis is on the process of relational co-ordination" (Gergen, 2009, p. 193).

In the earlier illustration with Bill and his father, my challenge was how to acknowledge his decision, at that moment, not to speak to me. Making a useful connection with Bill was partly to do with upending the expectation he held that I would somehow make him talk when he did not want to. Instead of seeing this as "resistance," I chose to consider it a valuable self-protective move on Bill's part. It was sensible not to divulge experiences to a relative stranger. For some clients, an immediate impression is formed about whether to trust a therapist but with many children brought, sometimes against their will, to seek help, the building of trust can be a more incremental process.

Connecting with clients is like a dance of intimacy, and each young person and family member will have their unique measure of the degree of emotional connection that will feel safe to them. This delicate appraisal of how to connect appropriately with each client will be illustrated in the practice examples throughout the book and focused upon in detail in Chap. 6. Wampold's (2015) research found that clients make up their minds quite quickly as to whether they can trust a therapist, so the initial meeting is a congress of similarities and differences, and with Bill the dance of intimacy was begun by accepting his wish not to contribute.

Aside: I worked for many years in South Wales with families from "the Valleys," working-class, closely-knit mining communities. I am Scottish and was brought up in a working-class housing estate in Glasgow. I came to appreciate that an indication of whether I'd be trusted enough by my clients was when a family member would enquire about my Scottish origins and occasionally say, "Do you know who you remind me of? .... Billy Connolly!" Billy Connolly is an internationally famous and popular Scottish comedian who comes from my home city and whose accent is like mine. Each time I would hear this comparison I felt confident I'd been provisionally accepted by the family through their teasing comparison with someone in the entertainment world they liked and respected. It was a cultural connection, a class connection, and based on our different experiences of Scottish/Welsh Celtic history.

We notice and respond to similarities and differences in meeting with others, and sometimes random elements, unknown to us, will affect how we are seen. What is required is versatility in finding steps that are more likely to connect with children and families we meet. We improvise each time.

More will be said about the intricate indicators of connecting with clients in the following chapters. Here it is important to emphasise that all therapeutic practice is a multi-sensorial relational engagement with our clients. We use thoughts, feelings, observations, smells touch and sound to inform how to proceed.

The detailed case examples that follow in Chap. 5 expand on these core ideas about facilitating change. In the next chapter, I outline some steps to help develop useful collaborative conversations with children and young people. I set out tips to help the practitioner in preparing to meet children in individual and family sessions. They are compiled from frequent questions often posed to me when I provide workshops on this topic.

References

Cecchin, G., Lane, G., & Ray, W. (1994). *The cybernetics of prejudices in the practice of psychotherapy*. Karnac.

Dallos, R., & Draper, R. (2010). *An introduction to family therapy: Systemic theory and practice.* Open University Press.

Fisch, R., Weakland, J., & Segal, L. (1982). *The tactics of change: Doing therapy briefly*. Jossey-Bass.

Freire, P. (1996). *Pedagogy of the oppressed.* Penguin.

Freire, P. (1998). *Pedagogy of freedom*. Rowman & Littlefield.

Gergen, K. J. (2009). *Relational being: Beyond self and community.* Oxford University Press.

Heimann, C. (2009). Guardian guide to performance, 9 May. *Guardian News and Media.*

Hoffman, L. (2002). *Family therapy: An intimate history*. W.W. Norton.

Santi, M. (Ed.). (2010). *Improvisation: Between technique and spontaneity.* Cambridge Scholars Publishing.

Shepherd, R., Johns, J., & Taylor Robinson, H (eds) (1996). D. W. Winnicott: Thinking About Children. London. Karnac.

Wampold, B. E. (2015). How important are the common factors in psychotherapy? An update. *World Psychiatry, 14*(3), 270–277.

Wilson, J. (2003). *Kindorientierte Therapie: Ein systemisch-kooperativer Ansatz.* Carl-Auer-Systeme Verlag.

Wilson, J. (2013). A social relational critique of the biomedical definition and treatment of ADHD: Ethical, practical and political implications. *Journal of Family Therapy, 36*, 6–19.

Wilson, J. (2017). *Creativity in times of constraint: A practitioner's companion in mental health and social care.* Routledge.

3

Meeting Children and Young People: Steps Towards Co-Creative Practice

Change is based on lived experience. In and of itself understanding, explaining, or narrating something is not sufficient to bring about change … An event must be lived with feelings and actions taking place in real time, in the real world, with real people in a moment of presentness.
—Stern (2004, p. xiii)

I set out in this chapter a series of steps which I have found useful when embarking on meeting children on their own and in family therapy sessions. The steps are not exclusive to those trained in family therapy; rather, they are ideas and techniques that have application across many professional contexts and disciplines and you, dear reader, are of course at liberty to take from these tips what fits your style of work.

Systemic practice is a search for connections that promote fresh opportunities for overcoming problems experienced by the child or family. It is not a template to tell people what to do (unless they would find this helpful). It is aimed at co-creating possibilities with clients. Similarly, in applying this principle to this book, the aim is to be in conversation with you rather than instructing you on what you need to do. If I should set

J. Wilson, *Building Creative Therapeutic Relationships with Children and Young People*,
Palgrave Texts in Counselling and Psychotherapy,
https://doi.org/10.1007/978-3-031-85706-5_3

out a series of steps to follow a protocol the last step is to tell the reader to avoid falling in love with protocols!

The steps are not intended as a lineal progression; however, for the sake of clarity I have sequenced them as a series of steps. Each step focuses on conditions that help to make the best of beginnings in meetings with children who are experiencing distress. Like all general tips they require amendment for each unique encounter.

Learning to Decentre

The term "decentring" was coined by Margaret Donaldson, Professor of Developmental Psychology, to describe our capacity to move outside our tendency to take a self-centred perspective towards others. To be self-centred in Donaldson's terms is "the act of looking out on the world from one's own position in it, literally or metaphorically and failing to realise how the same world, seen from a different stance, would appear- or what meaning the same words ,heard and interpreted by a different brain with a different store of previous knowledge and experience, would carry" (Donaldson, 1978, p. 18).

For the systemic practitioner the capacity to decentre involves imagining how each child or family member may view coming for therapy. For example, some children feel that having a social worker in their life is stigmatising or they fear they will be taken away from their parents and placed into foster care. Some clients of a psychology or psychiatric service may even harbour fantasies or fears that the therapist can read their minds! Decentring helps establish an orientation to practice that humanises the interaction. While manuals are useful in creating structure for therapeutic practices, the manuals should always be HUMANualised to ensure the practitioner makes a connection with children thatavoids any temptation to reduce conversation to a discussion of a child's diagnosis or problems without first making a connection with the personhood of the child.

Aside: One colleague presented a "case" to me for discussion in a clinic, describing in detail possible diagnoses of a ten-year-old boy based on previous reports she had gathered for the case presentation. She had met the boy on one occasion and wanted to know what action she should take next. She proceeded to rapidly outline the child's behaviour problems, his previous dealings with the child psychiatric service, and the various diagnoses that were more than likely to fit his profile. She proposed that the child's behaviour suggested he should be referred for further assessments for Attention Deficit Hyperactivity Disorder (ADHD), Autistic Spectrum Disorder (ASD) and signs of Obsessive Compulsive Disorder (OCD). All these abbreviations for psychiatric disorders were tripping off the tongue of the colleague who, when asked the child's name, had to refer to her notes. When one looks only with a microscopic level of detail on behaviours that may fit psychiatric categories, one misses the wider landscape of a child's life. For some children, a diagnosis of ADHD may prove helpful, but this is not the full picture, and it does nothing to enhance the focus on the life of a child. By only focusing on the diagnosis, the practitioner reduces the complexity of the narrative about the child and restricts her field of vision about options to help and resources to pursue. When time is tight and practitioners are caught in a whirl of activity, the language of objectification can become louder.

The Importance of Preparation and Planning

Preparation emphasises one's ability to be open and ready to respond to a child when they meet you. It involves a degree of spontaneous responsiveness (John Shotter personal communication) geared more to the present moment in a session rather than following a prescribed set of actions and steps set out beforehand.

In practice, preparation and planning are complementary components in readying oneself for a session. The main distinction is to notice when we are in one or another position. Here are a few tips that I have found useful to reflect on my responses to my clients and keep decentring uppermost in my mind in preparing to meet children and families.

Where possible, I have found it extremely useful to spend five or ten minutes before a session simply focusing on the impressions I gained from my previous sessions with a child. I check in with my own feelings about my coming session:

- Am I bored/expectant/anxious (more than usual)/curious about the direction the therapy might take? How do these pre-session feelings and thoughts offer useful ideas to ready myself for the coming meeting?
- What themes/topics were addressed in the previous session that generated fresh possibilities?
- What themes/topics failed to develop any creative possibilities?
- What were the matters that seemed important to the child that I failed to address?
- What do I think the child/family will wish from me in the coming session?
- Have family members indicated "No Go" areas for conversation, and what makes these matters difficult to talk about?

These and other reflective questions help me to anticipate the coming session without being drawn into dictating how it should proceed. The capacity to decentre is our ability to anticipate how best to make a useful connection with our clients as if seeing the world through their eyes and, in particular, how each client may be experiencing the meetings with a therapist.

Planning to follow a set procedure or protocol can be necessary where the practitioner's duty is to carry out checks on a child's degree of risk. Even in such clear interviewer-led procedures it is important for therapists to be mindful of the impact of following a procedure too tightly, such that the connection with a child is lost. If we lead too much from the front, we may find our young clients pull back from us.

For example, if therapists are overly anxious to follow a given plan, the tendency is to structure a session in such a way that instead of making a human connection, the clients feel processed as passive respondents to the questions of the practitioner. This often leads children and family members to feel objectified, instead of engaged in a constructive dialogue.

When a plan of action for a session leads to reluctance to participate on the part of a child or family, the danger is in pursuing the set plan despite the client's disengagement with the therapist. This difficulty can be countered by redirecting the initial focus of the meeting towards establishing a rationale for meeting together. This change of focus also helps to avoid too much initial talk of what is wrong or problematic before a safe enough context for meeting has been created.

Tip: Address apprehension about meeting as a family. Some questions and statements to consider:

- Asking each participant's views on coming to a session. For example, *"I would hope to appreciate each person's point of view so I can be of use to you and your family"* or *"I hope to try to get a picture of you and your family so I can be useful in our meeting. Usually, people have different points of view, so I hope to be able to pay attention to each person's words."*
- Asking about each person's wishes for a useful/successful outcome to the session.
- Noticing any reluctance to participate and giving this respectful attention and validation. One might say for example,
- *"Many children I have met are, quite rightly, a bit nervous/unclear/even worried about meeting someone they don't know. That is very understandable. I have only two rules for meeting. The first is that no one should talk about anything they do not wish to discuss and, secondly, if I ask you a question or say something that is too difficult to answer, please tell me."*
- Explaining your rationale for meeting the child / family. For example:
- *"By meeting with you as a family, I hope we can put our heads together to help figure out ways to help."* The practitioner is also noting who gives permission to speak, who remains silent, who looks apprehensive. To connect with each person present involves a form of conducting a session that is attentive to each person's engagement with one another and with the practitioner.

First Three Steps in the Conversation: Connect, Connect, Connect!!

Tip: Attend to the ways we listen

There are two basic modes of listening: listening in order to speak, and speaking in order to listen (Hoffman, 2002, p. 247). The distinction between these two modes can help us to be clearer about how we choose to respond in the ebb and flow of conversation. If I lead the conversation too far ahead of my young clients I fail to take account of the young person's hesitation or reluctance to follow my lead.

The one who speaks in order to listen is saying, in effect, "After you!" When we are silently listening to another person we can more readily "enter into the rhythm of the speaker's thought and experience that rhythm as language" (Freire, 1998, p. 104).

Tip: When anxious or unsure about working directly with children, do not be tempted to use formulations that provide a "convenient" rationale to avoid meeting with a child

In training family therapists over many years, it has become increasingly necessary to help trainees not to "fall in love" with various formulations about family dysfunction that could exclude children from participating in sessions.

A child's problems may be accurately viewed as an indicator of a wider, more serious, parental or marital problem, or as distracting attention from other structural problems in the family.

Whilst structural formulations can be very useful in helping to understand a child's difficulties in this wider context, therapists who are reluctant to meet with children may be drawn to formulations that focus attention away from the child onto other matters such as a presumed marital problem when the main issue is the therapist's reluctance to meet directly with children.

Children can be messy in sessions and not behave in ways that fit practice protocols. They may disrupt conversation, and may play by their own rules in a family session (Grabbe, 2001). Instead of exploring new ways of developing skills in their practice, the reluctant practitioner chooses not to work with children because they either do not like this client population or they feel overwhelmed when trying to make a connection with them. Yet when children are absent, and all practice is mediated between adults, the child can become an object of study rather than a participant in the therapeutic process. When children refuse to participate it is still possible to have them in mind if a child-in-context focus is maintained (illustrated fully in Chap. 5).

Tip: Use supervision to reflect, discuss and revisit our prejudices about children and childhood

In addition to preparing ourselves before meeting a child or family, it is also important to consider our values and our prejudices about children and childhood since these may powerfully shape what we believe to be the correct ways of child rearing. Our class, gender, age and race will all colour the context of the practice and influence how we respond to each other. What our clients see when they look at us will similarly be influenced by these cultural, race and class perspectives.

We all have prejudices. These are the reverentially held values or preferred truths that can influence and shape how we interact with children. An exploration of our prejudices helps to clarify those values that can sometimes lead us to be too certain about therapeutic goals and how to achieve them (see Cecchin et al., 1994 for a full exploration). It is important to explore our prejudices, not as pathologies but as starting points to tackling certain views that may restrict useful connections with children. Not everyone will feel at ease in working with children and certain children may trigger negative feelings that spontaneously arise in initially meeting a child or young person, especially when one's best efforts to openly connect with a child are rejected.

For example, some practitioners may hold a strong view that children are always victims of circumstance and consequently fail to notice a child's agency in contributing to negative or damaging behaviours. However, children are neither saints nor demons so a therapist needs to examine whether he has become seduced by one of these stereotypes. Discussing one's feelings and reactions in supervision can help to reposition the therapist to reappraise their responses to a child. If my perspective and/or feelings are not helping me to make progress in my work, the onus is on me to change direction and revisit my responses towards my clients.

Aside: Recently a therapist came for supervision and mentioned that she was so preoccupied about a child in her practice that she dreamt about him. When this preoccupation and worry was explored it became evident that the therapist had come to believe that she was the only person the child would confide in. She had become his "saviour" partly through her deep concern for his wellbeing but also because she had failed to connect with other important people in the child's life or professional support network. We can lose sight of this wider network of relationships when we begin to feel solely responsible for a child's wellbeing. In this case supervision was useful in broadening the conversation to consider other potential resources in the professional network that helped the therapist to reposition herself as part of a wider resource for the child.

Tip: Address therapeutic impasses and consider a change of therapist

When I meet with children and young people, I am curious to try to connect with their lives in ways that show an appreciation of who they are. When I fail to do this, I am puzzled as to why I cannot make a connection with this young person. Sometimes a therapeutic alliance is not fully in place. The young person may be wary of me or simply dislikes seeing me, or I somehow do not manage to become curiously engaged with them. This response needs exploration in supervision and if an impasse prevails, despite our attempts, the young person may be better linked up with another therapist. No therapist is infallible or can meet creatively with every child he sees. If an impasse occurs in practice, it is important to discuss this in supervision and sometimes openly with the family since prolonging unproductive sessions with a young person is pointless. Professional pride should not stop therapists from calling a halt when they are failing (Coleman, 1985).

Fortunately, this is not a common occurrence, but it is a sign of professional responsibility to know when to discuss failing with a young person, and the reasons for possibly changing therapist. Here it is important not to imply blame on the part of the young person or to leave them thinking they must be an almost untreatable case! It is better to acknowledge that a fresh approach may be a good next step, and for the therapist to sensitively address his lack of ability in finding ways to help the young person progress. He can hint at relational features but avoid implying that the young person has let the practice flounder.

For example, one might say, *"I think we've tried different ways to help with your worries, but I don't think I'm helping much. I think we are going round in circles and when this happens it's usually because I'm not being much help to a young person. I've found it more useful (helpful) to think about whether a different therapist would be better for you right now. .... What do you think?"* This phrasing brings in the young person as a contributor to the exploration of unproductive interaction with the therapist. Sometimes this can even lead to a fresh impetus in the practice, and the impasse may dissolve.

Tip: Allow participants to speak or not to speak

Somewhere near the beginning of a session it is helpful to set out preferred ways of conducting the session (this step was briefly discussed above).

To reiterate, it is important for family members to know that you will invite each person's views but that no one should talk about matters they do not wish to discuss. This helps avoid the trap of parents expecting the therapist to "magically" get their child to talk about matters that they themselves have failed to address. Equally, it provides a relief to the child that the therapist isn't only going to be supporting the parent's point of view. The rule applies to all, and although the wording varies depending on the context, it should be something like this: *"You should only discuss matters that feel safe enough to talk about. ... It's the same for all of us. We need to feel it is ok to discuss matters that are important to us."*

Sometimes parents will whisper to a therapist as if the child is not able to hear what is being said, or, at times, the child becomes an object of conversation rather than a participant. At these points, a therapist needs to find ways to engage directly with the whispering or objectification. For example, *"Are your whispers to protect your child or indicate a too painful matter ... or is there another way to hear what you are struggling to say outright?"* On occasions when children feel objectified in the conversation, I try to challenge this pattern directly, perhaps reiterating the wish to be in touch with each person present. Making sure that a child is not the object of complaints and negativity is an important part of engagement, and figuring out how to do this without alienating the parents is tricky.

Tip: State simply your rationale for meeting a family

It often helps to return to a ground rule about hearing the words of concern inside the words of complaint (as already mentioned). Closing down a parent's contribution or prematurely interrupting a parent who is anxious and angry about their child's behaviour risks distancing the parent from the therapist. Here it is important to try to connect with a parent's desire to find ways to help solve problems and attend to their goal to improve their relationships with their child. Emphasising their concern, love and worry about their child, i.e. the emotional context of their words of complaint, can often allow the conversation to be grounded in a more emotionally positive frame even when very painful matters are being discussed. When a parent feels you appreciate their point of view it is often then possible to move the conversation to include others.

It is also important to explain to children,in age-appropriate language, your aim and your ways of working. Too often young children are brought to a therapist without any prior knowledge of why they are being included.

It is useful to convey an atmosphere of participation in the opening session with a family, emphasising the therapist's wish to appreciate each person's point of view and welcoming differences of opinion.

It can also be helpful to invite adults and siblings to offer their opinions about children being present in family sessions. For example:

- What is expected of your child's contributions in our conversation? (This may include a discussion about parental authority/etiquette about a child's voice being heard alongside adults/exploring values about appropriate and inappropriate topics of conversation in which a child should be present.)
- What are your views on inviting other children in your family to our sessions?

- Is it possible to listen to your child's point of view without feeling you need to defend yourself?
- How might we invite everybody's participation so that it feels safe enough to take part in our session?
- What are your views on coming to therapy (including views on a referring professional's recommendation). For example,
- *"What did you think of the doctor's recommendation that seeing me could be useful to your child?"*

These are sample questions to give a sense of the therapist trying to create a safe enough context in meetings between children and their carers/family. The questions aim to explore the theme of **how** to meet, addressing the process of joining one another in a session. Only once this is explored is it more likely that people will feel able to address their concerns and vulnerabilities.

Tip: Where Possible Make a bridge between parents and child. Listen to the music!

To create a safe enough space to meet with children and their family members, the practitioner is required to be even handed in dealing with each person's contributions in a session. This is a challenge particularly if parents are furious about their child's behaviours. The therapist needs to attend to the parents' affect and complaints about their child but not allow this mood to dominate a session. We must decide on how to hear "problem saturated descriptions" (after White, 2011) yet avoid being trapped by negativity. To do this, each of us has to find, in our own style, a way to hear the words of complaint and, at the same time, interrupt to engage in ways that connect with the parent's emotional expression in the words of complaint. I refer to this as the "music in the words of complaint."

A parent's frustration can be linked to feelings of failure in helping their child, or of a loss of intimacy, or fear for their child's safety, or anxiety that their child will hate them for trying to seek help. This "mood music" is heard by a therapist who listens to the tone and the expression in the parent's words of complaint. The therapist does well to convey an appreciation of this "music" rather than being drawn into a coalition with the parent against the child. In most family sessions, the key point, by far, is for each person to feel that the practitioner appreciates their position without accepting this as the only true perspective on the child.

Tip: Look for connecting themes

Engaging family members in a joint discussion that seeks resources, explanations, new narratives and fresh options is a theme linked to the central concerns of the family and their child's problem. This focus may alter in time, but in the early stages of connecting with a family it is problematic to move away too soon from the expressed concerns about a child. You need careful attention as to when to broaden the conversation to include other matters.

It can be quite useful to preface one's wider exploratory questions by saying something like: *"Can I just ask a wider question to help me get a picture of your family?" or "This might seem a bit irrelevant right now but is it ok to ask how you have so far tried to help John with his OCD behaviours?" Or "I can see it is important not to move away from your worries for your son. I don't want to do this either so I will return to your concerns. Right now, is it ok to ask some more about…?"*

To summarise, here is a simple series of steps to keep in mind in navigating a family session with a child present:

Firstly, try to hear each person's views on attending a session (including views on a referring agent's suggestion).

Secondly, try to elicit each person's aims and wishes for therapy to be useful.

Thirdly, try to hear the various accounts as to "what is the matter" without being trapped in repetitive complaints or problem-saturated narratives.

Fourthly, look for resources in the family and invite discussion on what family members have already tried to help alleviate a problem.

Fifthly, try, where possible, to allow time at the end of sessions to invite reflections and opinions on how the session was experienced.

Tip: Try to develop a "bilingual" approach to the spoken word

So often we do not consider how the meanings we wish to convey in our words may fly above the heads of young children in therapy sessions. If I become too adult focused in a session I will begin to talk only in the language of the adult and forget to "translate" words to help a young child understand what is being said. Often, asking parents to help me find the appropriate words allows me to reconnect with the young ones in the session.

Mother: *"What Mr Wilson is trying to say is that your tummy feels funny and that makes you worried and need a hug from me."*
Me *"Thank you. That's a much better way of putting it!"*

Tip: Find a style of connecting that fits with the family's style

We should ask the question of ourselves: How can I find a suitable connection with the style of a family without succumbing to ways that fail to challenge their ideas when I need to? For example, some families are so noisy and vociferous that I seem to become a conductor of the session directing the traffic of conversation. This theme is explored in detail in Chap. 5.

With other families their very gentle style of talking "invites" me to become more of a jester, a gentle challenger of their too fragile sensitivities. In other words, helping to engage children in family sessions needs the orchestration of all participants, and the therapist is sometimes a follower and sometimes a leader. The skill is in sensing when and where to position oneself in relation to all those present. Supporting children in family sessions is not done at the expense of silencing the voices of all the others. The child's voice is part of the chorus that needs to be heard and appreciated if progress is to be made. The case illustrations in Chap. 5 develop this theme.

However, despite my best intentions, the above steps can sometimes fail to make the initial setting safe enough to continue.

Tip: What to do when co-operation is impossible

On the rare occasion that abusive arguments ensue, despite one's best attempts to create a safe enough context, the therapist also needs to give herself permission to stop a session that feels unsafe and potentially damaging to participants. This is an ethical decision based on the principle that therapy, as with any interaction, should not dehumanise participants. Sometimes, despite setting out the ground rules clearly, some family members may be so caught up in their anxiety or insecurity that they are not open to listening to what other family members have to say, especially when there is an extremely high level of tension between participants in a session. Here the practitioner may not manage to conduct a session without friction between family members bursting into inflammatory arguments. If this occurs, one option is to temporarily stop the session. Therapy can tolerate constructive argument, but when a context is uncontained no constructive practice is possible. This is an opportunity to pause and restructure how best to proceed.

An Imaginary Alternative to Consider: Young Arthur Revisited

Let us imagine, for one moment, revisiting Arthur at his home at the point when his father said that his son's injuries were due to "boisterous play." Let's assume that the atmosphere was intimidating for Arthur and for the visiting social worker. Let's also assume that Arthur looks apprehensive and glances towards his father when he hears him pronounce that Arthur's injuries were caused by playing too boisterously. In this alternative playback scenario, the practitioner notices the child's watchfulness and asks the father if he can talk for some minutes with Arthur alone.

The father reluctantly agrees to leave the room but looks over at Arthur on his way out as if to say, "Remember what I told you about being taken away if you tell what really happened." Under such silent intimidation Arthur would not be likely to talk with the social worker about his injuries, though the child's downcast and timid response would be, in effect, his unspoken words of distress and fear that, once fully appreciated, would mobilise the practitioner to take unilateral action on behalf of the boy.

This illustration depicts a scenario that highlights the distinction between an **investigative context** and a **more collaborative therapeutic setting** for practice. Therapists and social practitioners can sometimes become caught in failing to draw this distinction, either believing a therapeutic alliance is present when it is not or becoming investigative assessors of a family when a more collaborative relationship could be developed. The crucial point is in knowing which domain of practice we are entering (McCarthy & Byrne, 1988). In Arthur's case, the immediate need was to cease attending to the father's excuses for his son's injuries, and for the practitioner to act unilaterally on behalf of the child.

Usually, this task is not conducted by a lone social worker as in this imaginary construction. Support for social workers is crucial in such highly charged investigations and, as stated in Chap. 2, the relentless pressures and demands placed on social services mean due attention to detail can be overlooked, as was the case with Arthur.

Tip: Consider separate sessions for children and parents

This is an important consideration because excluding children from sessions is not to exclude them for your thinking or your concerns for their wellbeing. On occasion children benefit from sessions without their parents, and similarly parents can make good use of sessions without their children present. This is especially so if parents feel constrained not to hurt their child's feelings by expressing criticism of them or wish to protect them from certain painful topics. These can be legitimate reasons for requesting sessions without children taking part. However, seeing parents without their children can also run the risk of alienating the child from any direct contribution to the therapy.

Exploring the reasons for and consequence of meeting separately is important with the rationale set out clearly and where each member is aware of the bounds of confidentiality to be agreed upon. If parents insist that their child *must* be seen by you, there is little benefit in simply refusing to go along with this. I consider my response to such a request as an opportunity to join with the parents' concern to get help for their child. However, seeing a child for one or more individual sessions needs to be coupled with a clear aim of engaging the parents at a later stage in joint exploration. Exploring the reasons for individual sessions with their child is crucial, otherwise the parents may feel they have handed over their child's problems to you to somehow solve without their active participation.

When I meet a child on his own, I always try to keep in mind what matters can be discussed and fed back to the parents with the young person's co-operation. When very young children are seen on their own, where possible, I try to encourage the parents to observe my session and later comment on their observations by using suggestions like *"As parents you are the ears and eyes to help our work with your son" or "It's important for you (the parents) to be part of our team if we are to do a good job on behalf of your daughter."* In other words, the therapist tries to introduce the idea that the relational context of therapist, child and parents is the therapeutic medium, and that expertise resides in joint participation between us. However, simply saying this to parents who are convinced that their child needs an expert to "fix" him is unlikely to be accepted at first. So, the therapist must be constantly mindful of trying not to push parents to take part if this would lead to a withdrawal from therapy.

Tip: Learn to wait

If parents are apprehensive about taking part directly in sessions, we may have to wait until an opening arises perhaps when a parent feels safe enough to talk about their own vulnerabilities. For example, a parent may say, *"Well I also had a troubled childhood" or "I sometimes think I'm reacting in ways that make the problems worse" or "there's been so much tension lately, I think our child picks this up."* All these are examples of relational openings where the child's difficulties can begin to be considered in a wider context and where negative connotations, diagnostic categories and individual pathologies begin to hold less of a central position in the understandings of "what is the matter." In effect, the therapist is enacting the idea that expertise is contextual.

Aside: I recall a very anxious parent coming to see me in the psychiatric service about her depressed teenager. The mother, Linda, was adamant that Jane, her adolescent daughter, needed individual therapy, and no talk of family discussions would be entertained. As a response to her mother's insistence, Jane was first referred for art therapy, but she did not engage with the therapist. Next, she was referred for Cognitive Behavioural Therapy, but she failed to keep appointments. We were fast running out of options. At this point I asked if we could "try something different as your daughter is not making use of the one-to-one sessions. We need a change of direction … .. Something less predictable perhaps?" By this time Linda was becoming exasperated with her daughter and her apparent lack of engagement with our child psychiatric service. Reluctantly, she became more open to meeting me with all her children, and a family session was arranged. When I met with her children, I immediately noticed how enthusiastic Jane's two younger siblings were to talk with me. This gave me the idea that all three children could be my "team" to talk about the ways their mother, a single parent, had "already done a good job in the family." The children were effusive about their mother's abilities and strengths since their father died over a year before. Linda was asked to be a "reflector" to this mini session with her children and she was taken aback by her children's vote of confidence in her. This playfully serious family session helped cement our working alliance and cleared the way for family-based sessions that engaged all participants.

Clearly these playful means require sensitive handling, and the relationship between practitioner and family should be well established in mutual respect and shared good intention, otherwise such playful modes could be experienced as oppressive. They need a light touch from a therapist (for more detailed exploration of these and other modes for engaging families please see Wilson, 1998, 2007, 2017).

A young person must feel safe in this setting and trust the therapist enough not to break their confidence. At the same time this raises a further critical issue about one's ethical position. Just as childcare matters of abuse require action on behalf of the child to safeguard her, similarly the therapist may find that certain disclosures by a child may require a therapist to talk with parents about a serious matter, against the wishes of their child. There is no hard and fast rule here, but it is important not to avoid making known any matters that would be damaging to the child's welfare or place him at continued risk. This is an area that is best further explored in case-by-case discussion, but the basic point is that as therapists we are also citizens with responsibilities to uphold the rights of children and this cannot be compromised by an alliance with a child who continues to live in intolerable conditions.

To return to my initial description of Arthur Labinjo-Hughes, acting on behalf of a child requires statutory intervention and a legal system that upholds the rights of a child. Systemic practice is just as important in contexts of safeguarding children as it is in more co-operative styles of therapeutic engagement. These two domains, whilst different in engagement and direction, can nevertheless be considered within a systemic humanising orientation to practice.

Remember Co-Creativity and Co-Presence: Two Vital Features of Creativity in Practice

When working with young people who were depressed and suicidal, my practice was safer when trust and shared appreciation of their distress was coupled with an awareness that there could be better days ahead. The broader components of practice are also crucial here: risk assessments and links with key professionals, the child's school, family members and other important persons in the child's life. Being in touch with all the relevant contexts of the child's life helped to create a safer environment for my practice.

One element in creating a sense of safety in the practice is when there is a shared appreciation that the therapist holds the young person in mind between sessions. If a young person trusts the therapist to hold them in mind, my guess is that the young person may sense this. If mind is, indeed, a social relational phenomenon, then the young person and therapist are mutually "socially minded" in their therapeutic relationship. It is a circularity that is worth contemplating as an important dimension in practice. It is not that the therapist is overly preoccupied in thinking about a young person, more that feelings of care are present beyond the face-to-face meetings with the young person. Mutual trust, shared presence of mind and the ability to decentre are features that contribute to generating co- creativity between practitioner and client.

The above steps and tips are intended to help set the scene for a practice orientation that is, wherever possible, geared towards meetings with children in family sessions and/or on their own to generate useful dialogue between participants. An important orientation is for the practitioner to concentrate on the **psychosocial resources** of all participants, including those of the therapist. This orientation takes precedence over formulations that categorise or otherwise close down narratives about children to diagnostic formulations or where treatment programmes are implemented without due respect for the complexity of each child's situation and abilities. The job of the therapist is in creating contexts of possibility with their clients. This is an exploratory process which is playfully serious, at times irreverent and experimental but grounded in theoretical study and reflexive, critical thinking. The theoretical and philosophical influences are embedded in an orientation to practice that is anti-oppressive without being dogmatic, and first and foremost a process of mutual humanisation (Freire, 1996; Wilson, 2017). These matters are returned to in detail in Chap. 7.

In the next chapter I turn my attention to features that can help expand the repertoire of practice with children, as well as those conditions that would stifle co-creative practice. Each of us has our unique style in terms of how to practise and we will already have familiar methods and techniques regarding what to do in practice. This is our skills repertoire, and it can always be extended. The more we extend our repertoire the more likely we are to engage creatively with the children we meet.

References

Cecchin, G., Lane, G., & Ray, W. (1994). *The cybernetics of prejudices in the practice of psychotherapy*. Karnac.

Coleman, S. (Ed.). (1985). *Failures in family therapy*. Guilford Press.

Donaldson, M. (1978). *Children's Minds*. London: Fontana.

Freire, P. (1996). *Pedagogy of the oppressed*. Penguin.

Freire, P. (1998). *Pedagogy of freedom*. Rowman & Littlefield.

Grabbe, M. (2001). Kooperationmit Kindernin Therapieund Beratung. In A. von Schlippe, G. Losche, & C. Hawellek (Eds.), *FruhkindlicheLebenswelten und Erziehungsberatung. DieChancendesAnfangs* (pp. 220–242). Votum.

Hoffman, L. (2002). *Family therapy: An intimate history*. W.W. Norton.

McCarthy, I. C., & Byrne, N. O. (1988). Mis-taken love: Conversations on the problem of incest in an Irish context. *Family Process, 27*, 181–199.

White, M. (2011). *Narrative practice: Continuing the conversation* (D. Denborough, Ed.). Norton.

Wilson, J. (1998). *Child focused practice: A collaborative systemic approach*. Karnac.

Wilson, J. (2007). *The performance of practice: Enhancing the repertoire of therapy with children and families*. Karnac.

Wilson, J. (2017). *Creativity in times of constraint: A practitioner's companion in mental health and social care*. Routledge.

4

Exploring the Repertoire of Practice: Methods, Opportunities and Constraints to Creativity

While concepts help us to think critically about how to be involved in practice, ideas alone are not enough. We also need to find ways to translate them into words and actions that engage interest and curiosity. Family therapists are trained in versions of the "talking cure" but with young children, the language of play and performance is a mode that may more easily engage their curiosity.

Research into younger children's views of therapy (Stith et al., 1996) suggests that pre-adolescent children prefer a combination of play and action, along with talking. Most children identify positively with therapists who are warm and personable and, importantly, meet with them as an equal in their eyes. Talking down to children is a big mistake. Children also view family meetings as useful so long as they are not the only focus of attention (Wilson, 1998, 2003). Some children actively wish to be included in sessions and may become anxious if excluded from family sessions. They may worry about their parents if they appear unhappy and prefer to participate in discussing what ails their family. Most importantly, they appreciate having their opinions aired and taken seriously. Therapists do not need to become children's "entertainers" but it is worth

J. Wilson, *Building Creative Therapeutic Relationships with Children and Young People*, Palgrave Texts in Counselling and Psychotherapy,
https://doi.org/10.1007/978-3-031-85706-5_4

considering how to develop some additional skills in meeting with children through more playful means, and these are set out below. Curiosity, like creativity, is considered a relational process, and for the following modes to be useful, they must emerge in the mutuality of the responses between all participants. (The case illustrations in Chap 5 amplify this relational focus.)

A word of caution: Not all children will feel at ease with a therapist's warm and sensitive manner, since some children who have experienced abuse and trauma may perceive such warmth as untrustworthy, even frightening. The therapist must adapt to a level of intimacy that is safe enough for the child and extend his repertoire of ways to find creative connections with each child. Chapter 6 will look in detail at the flow of moment-to-moment feelings and actions by a therapist that can help in building creative relationships with children and their families. The main aim is to create the conditions within which children become curious about taking part in a relationship with a therapist that is neither intrusive nor overly directive.

Modes of Connection: Looking Into the Systemic "Playground of Practice"

Imagine you are observing young children playing at break time in the playground. Some may be involved in animated chatter, one child may be singing, another skipping, one stands quietly daydreaming, whilst another is engrossed in a computer game. Two children are creating some artwork and others are playing a game together, one is reading a book, another telling a story. We see children using their imagination; they are improvising through pretence and make believe and by doing so they are contributing to their knowledge and growth.

Since our aim here is to enhance possibilities for connections with children, the repertoire of practitioners can be extended into more playful domains described below, without losing sight of the systemic concepts that inform purposeful creative practice (see also Wilson, 2007).

- **The importance of attending to our physical movements in sessions**: moving between participants; changing seating, playing on the floor; outdoor sessions that include activities like walking or playing games. For example, "busy" children, often diagnosed with ADHD, are more likely to respond to action-oriented interaction with a therapist than being expected to sit in a therapy room chair for a long time. A simple step is to make available age-appropriate toys for children in the therapy room; some toys placed to the side of the direct conversational space allows young children to move to the margins yet remain involved. In addition, I have found that specially selected toys in the middle of the room allow more direct presence of a child without overly focusing on them. Toys that a child had been drawn to in previous sessions should be made available each time. This is a small welcoming gesture that can help settle a child in a session. We can also move out of the therapist's chair. This seems such a simple move but so many family therapists seem wedded to sitting in a chair and primarily asking questions, some more suited to adult conversation. A therapist's creative repertoire is enhanced by deliberately getting out of the chair to make connections with family members. It can be a challenge to some therapists trained in sedentary ways of interviewing to realise that the language of connection also includes movement—safe physical closeness or touch, gestures to enrich the intended message in the spoken word and voice tone to suit the emotional atmosphere of a session. These are all part of the language of connection with another. In working with children, it is important to include means to engage that are age and developmentally appropriate for each child and young person. Sitting in chairs may be the most appropriate position to take but not at the expense of trying out new moves for fear of embarrassment.
- **Engaging in forms of the written and spoken word**: letters to absent family members, reading poetry, and using song lyrics and journal articles are all potential means to open conversations on important matters that connect with a child's perceived problems and resources. (The case example of Yasmin in Chap. 5 includes an illustration of composing a letter to an abusive family member.) Stories written or narrated can be co-authored with children or other family members (see also White and Epston (1990), White (2011) and Wilson (2007, 2013).

Below is a detailed case example illustrating steps involved in creating a custom-built story based on my direct experience of working therapeutically with a family. The story is a link in the chain of connections with a family and is designed to promote more generative dialogue and positive steps for the family involved.

The Background to the Story

Billie is a seven-year-old girl who is brought to see me by her mother Michelle. Michelle is blind in one eye following a brutal assault by her male partner some nine months earlier. Billie witnessed her mother's beating and, according to Michelle, Billie said she wanted to "clear up the blood to make it better." Michelle's ex-partner was imprisoned for the assault, and Michelle and Billie left the area where they had lived to seek anonymity in a small town in Wales.

In the initial meetings with the mother and Billie I could see how timidly Billie behaved. I was concerned that the mother's understandable urgency to get help for her daughter was geared towards getting Billie to talk about her painful experiences. I also learned that Michelle had begun to make a new life for herself and her daughter.

The idea for composing a story to help begin a more paced and sensitive engagement came to me when Billie told me about taking her pet goldfish with her when she and her mother had to leave to come to their new home. Her care for the goldfish offered me a beginning connection with the child and the kernel of an idea for the following story.

The Focus and Context of the Story

A story has an author, or authors, an audience and a central focus. In this case, my aim was to convey more appreciation of how both mother and daughter were dealing with the effects of their painful experiences. To do this required me to offer a safe enough form of narrative that would hopefully engage their curiosity and ring true to their experience without exposing their vulnerabilities too starkly.

Too painful a narrative would only make Billie feel fearful. Too positive a story would avoid the painful experiences felt by the child and her mother. Creating a story allows for the possibility of expressing painful and sensitive matters in an "as if" form, a safe distance from the actual experience yet allowing Billie and her mother an opportunity to identify with the characters portrayed.

The content of the story was garnered from my conversations with Michelle and Billie and key elements of their story told to me. I listened to the descriptions of the mother's experience of her departure from her life in England and her desire to build a new life for Billie and herself. She talked of her new home and of Billie attending a new primary school. The experiences of being abused by her previous partner were near the surface in the early sessions but not expanded upon. I could see how apprehensive Michelle was about her tentative new beginnings. I also felt that part of Michelle's motivation to seek help was her guilt at what Billie had witnessed, shame at what had happened in her life, and a haunting apprehension about what the future might hold.

These were some of the impressions and details that provided the content of the story. My aim was to include the matters that were difficult to voice directly. I employ an additional device, ***the voice of the writer***, where I make comments on the reasons for the characters' responses. These comments, bracketed in italics, are intended as small meta comments as the story develops. In form they are similar to a therapist's reflections during an interview with a family where the yet unspoken but implicit themes may begin to be expressed.

Setting the Scene

The story I drafted was first read by Michelle to seek her approval and make any amendments she might suggest. She accepted the following version and chose to read the story to Billie in instalments.

The story was printed in colourful book form for Billie with an illustration on the front cover of two goldfish in a bowl.

Melissa The Goldfish: A Story for Billie (see also Wilson, 2007)

Melissa was a very pretty, young fish. She was a goldfish. She swam around in her goldfish bowl quite happily, in and out of the pretend seaweed, playing with her mother, Samantha. Samantha was a proud and beautiful goldfish. She and Melissa would enjoy swimming around each other, looking at the world outside from their goldfish bowl.

> (Have *you ever imagined what a goldfish sees when she looks out from a goldfish bowl? She probably sees funny shapes of people and television sets and wonders what everyone outside is doing.)*

One day Melissa and her mother were having a bite to eat (ants eggs seemed to drop in from the sky as if by magic).

Suddenly there was an almighty splash! and a very handsome new goldfish appeared. He had a black line down his back, and silvery fins. After being surprised by him Samantha and Melissa got on very well with this new, handsome Silvey Prince (as *they decided to call him).* They began to like him; he made them laugh and life inside the goldfish bowl was good…

One day, however, when they were all swimming around, the Silvery Prince said. "This goldfish bowl is too small, and you (pointing to Samantha and Melissa) are taking up too much room!"

Samantha and Melissa were shocked and frightened. Their goldish eyes opened very wide, and their mouths opened even wider.

Before Samantha could tell the Silvery Prince that this was her bowl, and belonged to no one else, he whacked her so hard with his tail that she flew against the side of the bowl and hurt her fins very badly. She lay there and couldn't get up. Melissa was very frightened. (*It was the kind of fright where you don't really know what to say or what to feel. You just know that something wrong has happened, and you don't like it.)*

Melissa wanted it to be all better again. She wanted the goldfish bowl to be a happy place once more. She wanted the Silvery Prince to be nice again, to be good to her and her mum. She wanted him to like her because deep down inside she liked him very much, and he was good fun at times.

But this was a bad thing he had done, and she didn't understand it for one minute.

Slowly Samantha got up and began to swim again. It took a while, and she was always frightened about what the Silvery Prince might do next. For a long time, Samantha and Melissa said nothing to each other. They just kept themselves hidden behind the pretend seaweed. The Silvery Prince swam around like he was the King of the sea.

Melissa and her mum were very unhappy. They showed this by keeping very quiet or sometimes getting very, very angry and flapping their tails around. But they didn't cry like human beings do (*maybe, because tears are made from water, we can't tell when a goldfish cries).*

Anyway, one day there was another big splash. This time when Melissa and Samantha opened their eyes the Silvery Prince was gone. At first Samantha and Melissa couldn't believe it. They breathed a big sigh of relief through their gills, and began to swim out slowly, further and further from behind the pretend seaweed, until they began to feel a little bit more at home again. Samantha said, "I wonder where he has gone?"

"I hope he has gone for good!" said Melissa "I never want to see him again. He was so bad to you. He should never have bashed you with his tail and hurt you so much. This our bowl. It has always been *our* bowl. Why do you think he spoiled everything?"

Samantha couldn't find the words to explain to her daughter. She too had found the Silvery Prince someone she liked very, very much. In goldfish language she said to herself, "How is it possible to like someone so very much and yet he should do such bad things? This is very confusing." It made her swim round and round in frantic circles trying to make sense of this.

Slowly over the following goldfish weeks and months, and a goldfish year, Melissa and Samantha began to feel safer again, but they always had one big question that worried them. (*Do you know what this was? It was this: Would there be a time, sometime in the future when there would be a big splash, and the Silvery Prince would come back again?*) This was frightening for Samantha and Melissa. (*Sometimes when people are frightened, they think it is best not to talk about the frightening thing, and I can understand that because we all try to forget frightening things.)*

As Melissa swam around the goldfish bowl, she said to herself, "I wonder: if I had been nicer to that Silvery Prince would he have liked me better and liked my mum better? Maybe I made him do something to hurt my mum, but I can't think what that would have been. Maybe if I had shared my food a bit more or let him swim a bit more behind the pretend seaweed. ... Even though I am angry about what he did, sometimes, just sometimes, I would like to hear how he is doing and if he is unhappy. I wonder if he is in another goldfish bowl on his own, or if he has a friend? I wonder what he looks like now. I wonder if he still has the silvery gills and the black line down his back. I wonder if I will ever see him again without being frightened."

Melissa's mum sometimes felt sad about the things that had happened. She even thought, "Maybe I have myself to blame. If only I'd kept him away from us. If only I had spoken to him a bit more strongly. If only I had seen that he wanted to take over our goldfish bowl, maybe Melissa wouldn't be so upset." She wanted to tell Melissa how much she loved her and how sorry she was that bad things had happened to her.

Some good things began to happen too: the goldfish bowl was beginning to look smart again. The water was calm. They could breathe through their gills more easily. Samantha had made some special plans. She was becoming a stronger goldfish. Melissa liked that. She could see there was a quickness now in the way Samantha patrolled the goldfish bowl and slowly, slowly at first, Melissa began to play again. She began to pick up little pebbles and play with them in the bowl. She began to dart in and out of the pretend seaweed like she used to do. She began to want to have some more friends again. She remembered that goldfish swim around in big groups, and when she started to think of this, she felt good. Her tail would flick a little bit, and she would dart around the goldfish bowl. She could see, slowly at first, that things over the last goldfish year were beginning to feel safer.

This is the end of this part of the story of Melissa. There could be more adventures and things to say but this is Melissa's story so far. What do you think could happen next, I wonder...?

Tip: On creating stories for (and with) children and family members

In workshops on creating stories with and on behalf of children, I am often met with participants' reticence in believing they are not creative enough to author stories. Yet, with a few simple rules in place, participants free themselves up to experiment, to play and to use their imagination. It's as if permission is granted to enjoy the exploration in play albeit for particularly important and serious matters.

Put simply, here is a brief framework to consider.

1. Engage and explore a child's interests and strengths, and their positive relationships with family members, friends and pets as these help to provide source material for the story.
2. Learn from a child's impressions upon you, from their ways of talking, gestures, facial expressions and their general demeanour as this helps create the tone of the story. For example, whether to include light touches, occasional jokes or keep the tone serious. These observations and impressions help to shape the narrative and engage a child's curiosity.
3. Use your imagination to consider the child's central concerns/fears/worries that you glean from your meetings with the child and family. These elements will be introduced sensitively into the storyline as above with Billie and her mother.

These tips help in preparing for the reflections that will be woven into the plot of the story. The story maker adds to the storyline by including sensitive reflections informed by systemic thinking, a relational focus and one's embodied responses during the interactions with the child and family.

The story is not an end point. It is part of the ongoing connection with the child and family. It is important to encourage feedback on the story where appropriate. Sometimes, however, stories are best left without further discussion. I have noticed that some children prefer undisturbed private reflection in order to make their own connection with the words that touch them. It is not always useful to unravel a storyline. A light inference may be enough to set a new train of thought in motion.

The Boy Who Lost His Words

A boy of nine was defined as an elective mute. He had said nothing to me in family sessions until his mother mentioned that he loved dogs and playing games on his computer. He communicated with others via his laptop, so I devised a story to send to him via his mother's email address. The story was about a dog who had lost its bark and set out to find it. As with the above tips I based the story on the dog feeling lost and anxious and its apprehension about barking, themes that impressed me when meeting with the child and his family. The boy liked the story, and a positive change occurred when the mother bought her son a puppy who became the boy's friend and confidante. His elective mutism waned after the puppy arrived in his life. My story was only one step in this more creative direction stimulated by his mother's initiative.

In other cases, the story can be critically examined to stimulate further useful discussion and new directions initiated by family members. The key is to judge the responses to the story by the child and family members and resist any temptation to overly direct the course of the conversation. The aim is to maintain curiosity and learn from a child's response which next step may be possible. Only when a therapist gains permission to offer a "guess" as to a child's feelings should this be done. Even then, the therapist needs to check with the young client if their guesses are accurate or require alteration.

- **Utilising Multimedia**

As in the vignette above, many children are skilled in using multimedia as a means of communicating and therapists can make use of texting, email and recommending websites that could assist them. The recent pandemic led many therapists to work online, and some children and young people reported that this mode of communication felt comfortable and less intrusive than face-to-face meetings with a therapist in a psychiatric clinic. Online home-based sessions are often easier to arrange, but overuse of online therapy has its limitations. Direct, in-room sessions provide a three-dimensional physically present experience of meeting that offers opportunities to use the physical space of a therapy room to create movements, literal and figurative, that can only be approximated online. We are literally more in touch when not mediated by the virtual context of on-screen discussions. When highly charged emotions are present, online practice cannot contain feelings, nor is the therapist able to immediately intervene when matters of safety demand attention. With reservations, online practice can be useful but should not be appropriated only to save time and money when face-to-face meetings are necessary (Wilson, 2021).

- **Include artwork and visual aids**

The use of figures to tell stories, graphic genograms to open connections with children, and drawings, card games, lists and quizzes to promote discussion (see Wilson, 1998) are all aids that some children can engage in, partly because they use such means in schoolwork with their teachers. These act as a joint focus for therapist and child and provide a useful way to explore events in a child's life where the spoken word alone is insufficient. Young children may use this form of play to express their "inner talk" safely in meeting with the therapist, for example, using figures to represent the child, and others. This representation allows the child to tell of their experiences more safely through the indirect, "third-person" figure, and thus helps make sense of complicated moves in their lives, for example devising "mini sculpts" to help children describe complex moves in their lives in foster care and associated feelings (for a detailed account see Wilson, 1998).

An Invitation to Step Outside Your Usual Repertoire

The Systemic Playground of Practice uses modes of play to enact practice underpinned by systemic theory and related approaches. ***It is not a separate form of therapy.*** The modes of play are specifically tailored to enhance useful connections with the young clients and include various forms of role play, role reversals, therapist as child's "inner talk," family members as child's inner talk, reflecting team as role play family members, and family members as reflecting team (see example below and Wilson, 2007 and 2017 for further detailed examples). The main point here is to create flexibility in one's positioning as a therapist. We are playing within the context of family therapy and altering more common modes of practice to generate more creative connections together with the families and children we meet (see Wilson, 2016). What matters is the therapist's willingness and freedom to experiment. Below is one example from the Systemic Playground of Practice where singing helped make a connection with a young girl in residential care.

In workshops on therapy with children, I often ask participants to volunteer examples of effective practice in their repertoires. However, I also ask them to give examples that have not been discussed before now as they feared that colleagues would be critical of their practice, considering the example as outside the accepted protocol of their profession. Over the years this question has always provoked creative responses from participants, as if they finally realised that spontaneous moments that helped children were at last being recognised, even applauded.

Below is an example of such spontaneous responsiveness (Shotter, 2016) in which the therapist's singing became a turning point in establishing a therapeutic connection with a young person (See also Wilson, 2007).

The Sound of Music *and the Moment of Connection*

The head social worker of a residential home for children based near Dublin provided this illustration of "Doing Something Outside The Box" in response to the question "Have you ever done anything unusual and effective but did not talk to colleagues about it for fear of their criticism, or of it sounding 'off the wall'?"

The social worker described how she and her colleagues were puzzled and feeling at a loss in their supportive attempts to talk with a teenage girl in their care who refused to talk to anyone in the staff group or other children in the residential home. The girl had been received into care some six weeks earlier and had a history of elective mutism. The social worker and her colleague had taken the girl to her hometown to review her progress in care. No words were offered by the girl on the car journey south over the Wicklow hills. On the way back to Dublin, the evening sun was shining and the view from the top of the Wicklow hills was so impressive that the head social worker stopped the car to appreciate the view.

All three stood together watching the sun setting behind the hills. At a certain moment the social worker recalled the film *The Sound of Music* featuring Julie Andrews singing "The Hills Are Alive"." The social worker turned to her colleague and began to sing (to the tune of the song, and in the style of Julie Andrews) "Why will she not talk to us?" Her colleague replied in kind, "I don't know why she will not talk to us!". The girl burst out laughing and this proved to be the beginning of more open connection between the head social worker and the young person.

Sometimes we work on a hunch because it comes to us and it seems worthwhile though we have not, at that moment, figured out quite what has prompted our response. It just "feels right at the time." Reflection in action is a skill to be honed and at times our spontaneous response can also be trusted.

I am not advocating a random ill-considered spontaneous response; it is more accurately a spontaneous response benignly intended and drawn from one's reading of the positive connection with the client. I am here indicating that taking a considered risk can be useful. Sometimes our rationale for our actions comes after the fact since not all practice is capable of thorough reflection-in-action (Schon, 1986). Our guide is our ethical concern and care for the client, an attitude of humility, and an ability to step outside usual patterns of communication when they have become redundant.

Playing Seriously with Established Methods

Here is an example of broadening the possibilities in adapting a reflecting team format to introduce a playfully serious element to practice (see also Wilson, 2007, 2017).

A Little Background

The use of a team to observe practice became a feature of my family therapy from the early 1980s exploring the approach of the Milan school (Palazzoli et al., 1978, 1980a, 1980b). Later developments, primarily initiated by Tom Andersen and colleagues (Andersen, 1990), made the previously mysterious team "behind the screen" more visible. Families were invited to listen and observe the team's ideas and reflections. The observers were now the observed, and the one-way screen became a two-way linkup. So, instead of the family being subjected to a message (sometimes a strategically worded paradox), from an anonymous team behind a one-way mirror, they became participants in the ongoing series of reflections and dialogue.

This development promoted a more transparent and democratic attitude in family therapy sessions in which family members were more connected in conversation with the therapy team rather than being subject to interventions from an observing team (for a more detailed history on the development of teams in family therapy see Dallos and Draper (2010).

My practice over the last thirty years has allowed me to experiment with variations on collaborative reflecting team processes that further developed the definition of "team" to include family members and other significant people in a child's life. These alternative reflecting team structures led to a blurring of distinctions between client family and therapists. All were interested in offering reflections and sharing opinions. At the same time, I, as co-ordinating therapist, tried to keep an overseeing eye as an observer/ participant to ensure the focus on helping a family remain central to the reflecting teams' activities. Variations can be found in Wilson (2007)) and (2017) including: child as consultant to the therapist, playback therapy and the reflecting team as theatre. These family-plus-therapist reflecting teams can be useful in creating space for members to listen from a different position. Here is one example by way of illustration.

The Noisy Family and the Motivated Young Person

John, aged fourteen, was referred to the CAMHS service in Greenwich, London, for anxiety and depression. He was also taking drugs, and at risk of school exclusion. The first family therapy session was a noisy, combustible event with family members arguing with one another, and my role seemed more of a referee than a reflective therapist. However, despite the noise, this was a family that really cared for John, and I had made a good enough connection for them to return for a second appointment. They were just as noisy as in the first session but at the beginning the adults (maternal grandparents, mother and John's aunt) all wanted the second session to focus on John to hear more about his views. I asked John if he could agree to contribute his opinions in this session and he immediately agreed. This was the spark that led me into doing something different. I suggested that John and I make up "Team One." I proposed that I would talk with John for a time to hear more of his viewpoints but in addition I suggested the adults become "Team Two" in the room and, lastly, that my colleagues behind the screen would be "Team Three." John and I would begin by hearing of his concerns, and after a while we would invite Team Two and Team Three to offer their views.

However, John's family were not prone to silent listening and reflecting. They were lively, and conversation was often punctuated by interruptions, corrections, jokes, laughter and the occasional swear word. Still, I could see they were a close family, and they loved John.

I suggested that for family members to be a reflecting team it was necessary for them to sit in silence during my conversation with John. I explained that their focus was to notice how our conversation affected them, and to think how they might like to contribute later once John and I had discussed what he wanted to raise as his concerns.

John's mother was extremely challenged by my suggestion of sitting in silence. She said in a half joking manner that she found it impossible not to talk. We joked and negotiated that she would try to listen for perhaps ten minutes, and she agreed. The family members seemed intrigued, and they liked the idea of being a team that would contribute to helping

John. Similarly, my colleagues liked the novelty in the mode of the reflecting team. Now we were all together working on the stipulated focus of the family.

Aside: Sometimes using the term "reflecting team" does not fit the familiar language of a family, and in this case I asked family members to listen to John's opinions and later say what they would like to say and how they felt having listened to John. These were simple instructions to listen to their thoughts and attend to their feelings without jumping to conclusions or contradicting John while I talked with him. For this family this was a challenge, but remarkably, they agreed to become a "Listening Team."

The atmosphere changed as John talked about his worry for his mother and his wish to live with her again after many years of being looked after by his maternal grandparents. As our conversation continued uninterrupted, I sensed the stillness in the adult family members as they allowed themselves to listen and permit John's words to fill the room.

After some time, I invited the family "team" to offer their ideas and thoughts.

The grandparents talked movingly about how they took John to live with them after his mother gave birth to him when she was sixteen. The tone of their responses was quietly sensitive towards John and his mother in recounting this particularly important event in their family life. They used their "listening team" to open new conversation about the care of John and the anxieties he had about his mother's current living arrangements with a new male partner. This session created a closer working alliance with this family and although they continued to be argumentative in future sessions there was a firm grounding in being available for mutual listening. I became less of a referee. The therapy continued to explore these events in later sessions.

The point of this illustration is to underline the ways in which a playfully serious orientation to methods used in family therapy can lead to the emergence and development of fresh variants (see also Wilson, 2016).

Tip: On moving from an individual to a relational focus with families

Parents may come to therapy requesting a clear definition of what is the matter with their child. These requests may come from a belief that a problem resides inside a child and has little to do with relationships with others. Sometimes family members are desperate to have a clear diagnosis and treatment plan. As proposed in Chap. 2, their desperation, that is the "music" in the words of complaint, often comes from a desire to get clarity and a definitive description of a child's problems. A parent's wish to find solutions must be acknowledged and validated. There is no point in directly challenging the idea that a child's problems are genetic, biological, constitutional and require medical intervention. Clients can become wedded to a problem definition, and one cannot simply divorce them from this idea. The systemic therapist has to engage family members in ways that respect their opinions and at the same time try to widen the context to engage the family in further exploration. The key is to avoid getting stuck in "either/or" perspectives and instead entertain a "both/and" orientation in family sessions where possible. The systemic therapist's duty of care is to both help the child and explore relevant social relations that have a bearing on a child's life. This is not to deny the individual child's unique experience, or that certain features—a child's constitution, physical abilities or intellectual capacities—are irrelevant. They are crucial to the therapist's engagement with the child and their family. The main aim is to mobilise a family's resources to help in widening the frame of relevance in assisting in the family/individual therapy.

Taking Play Seriously Within a Systemic Theoretical Approach

In listing these modes, a question arises about whether our professional identities have somehow restricted the range of acceptable behaviours we allow ourselves to perform. Have we lost sight of the importance of humour, jokes, playful teasing of our clients? Has therapy become a restricted range of activities that shuts the door on freer expression in therapy? Are we convinced by those who would argue that to sing or play a musical game with a family is somehow not REAL therapy? Too much formality, or inappropriate informality, is a way to limit creativity in practice and distance us from the children we meet. But the presence of a playful mind in touch with serious intention is a combination that creates possibilities for practitioners to breathe new life into the repertoire of their practice.

All the foregoing examples are embedded in a systemic, relational theoretical framework and each method is conceptualised within a systemic orientation to practice. This is not limited only to a family therapy interview. This broad perspective takes into its vision the wider organisational structures and policies that determine, to a greater or lesser extent, what flexibility a practitioner may have to develop.

*Aside: A family therapist approached me at a workshop I was offering on systemic approaches to therapy with children. I had outlined many of the above modes for opening therapeutic connections with children, including showing a video of me playing on the floor of the therapy room with young children telling me a story of their loss of family connections through a mini sculpt (*Wilson, 1998*). The colleague was an experienced practitioner who previously practised as a play therapist for many years. In mid-career he decided to train as a family therapist and had put aside all his skills and knowledge as a play therapist, suspending them to learn more about the systemic paradigm.*

He was perplexed having seen my video of playing on the floor with the two boys. He told me that his Family Therapy training was vastly different from his previous ways of working such that he gave up all his play therapy methods when he became a family therapist. His encounter with me challenged this assumption and revealed how certain trainings can restrict options for creativity. He had lost touch with skills and modes of connecting with children from his previous job as a play therapist because they had not been legitimised in his family therapy training. He had not given himself permission to use his methods and ideas from his former profession to see what creative links could be made with his new systemic theorising and methodology. As a result, he was restricted in his repertoire of practice possibilities.

What was missing from his family therapy training was the inclusion of a systemic theoretical approach that embraced many different modalities to make connections with children and families. The theoretical perspectives between play therapy and family therapy differ. Modalities mentioned here are not owned by any one approach. What matters is HOW methods and techniques are employed and the meaning attributed to them. The impetus in playfully serious systemic practice is to use any method that proves effective. My mentor and source of inspiration, Gianfranco Cecchin, from the Milan Associates (Cecchin, 1987; Cecchin et al., 1992, 1994) used to say, "If the method is not working, change the method!" (personal communication). The forms of play in all these examples are conceptualised within a systemic, relational theoretical framework whilst the mode of practice is shaped to best connect with the child. We are again improvising a means to co-create new directions towards therapeutic outcomes.

Co-creativity is context dependant, and this next section focuses attention on the wider relational factors that are necessary to create the conditions for creative bridge building with children and families AND with colleagues.

Necessary Conditions for Maintaining Co-Creativity in Practice and Tackling Constraints

A few years ago, I led a series of training sessions in a Swedish mental health service in Kalmar, on the southeast coast of Sweden. The series was arranged by the health board to assist practitioners in their wishes to become more effective in their therapeutic work with children and families.

The series of six intensive training sessions took place over eighteen months. During this time, the Swedish psychiatric hospital was in the flow of several changes in structure and policy implementation. Services were being compartmentalised, specialisms were being created that separated practitioners from their colleagues, and there was an increasing requirement on time-limited contacts with patients. Further demands were being made to cut waiting lists, and there were more pressing procedures for recording statistics and outcomes. You may recognise some if not all of these demands in your service. However, while the impact of such policy requirements was important to acknowledge, it was also important not to get lost in feelings of hopelessness but to begin to address together what it *is* possible to do. It is a tricky balance to strike because often organisational pressures are at the front of practitioner's minds.

As the training sessions developed, practitioners were increasingly freed up to talk about their practice dilemmas and about how to work more co-operatively with each other. We had created a safe enough context to engage in discussion without recourse to unhelpful competition between disciplines. How had we managed to create this exploratory setting for learning?

Despite the organisational pressures, the course had been supported by the managers of the service so there was already a positive view towards the training being a useful part of the participants' work.

My aim was to make the course a safe enough place for trial-and-error learning. By showing my practice on video tape and role plays I was risking my resources. I made errors, invited feedback, valued participants similarly taking risks in exercises that "exposed" their practice to one another. It was important to teach the course in a way that was congruent with my means of conducting my practice. We entertained diverse opinions and we created a context based on curiosity towards learning, expanding one's skills repertoire. This book is a written exemplar of the general approach I take when providing workshops or running courses. The content may vary but the practice philosophy is consistent.

The teaching style avoids a "top-down" relationship with participants. Humour and serious learning go hand in hand. Without the warmth of humour in a learning context the atmosphere can become dry and make participants less inclined to try out new ways of working. It was important to view participants as competent professionals, and my job was to open new routes for their practice to develop further.

The teacher learns from the student about how best to create the conditions to learn, and the words of the beginning quote from Kailash Satyarthi echo here. A childlike attitude is required to allow oneself to be open to new learning, and the participants on the Swedish course created this opportunity with me. The trainer acts as a conduit to help participants take a risk and open themselves to new learning. The effect of this atmosphere for learning perhaps enabled the participants to warm to exploration of their repertoires.

At one point I asked the group to consider what features of their working context would promote fresh creativity in their practice. They produced the following suggestions which were subsequently built into their organisational structure with the help of their management team. They decided to implement more joint working, more time for supervision of clinical process (not simply case management supervision), more time built in to discussing collegiate relationships, especially if tensions are arising, and more openness in all aspects of their practice. One participant stated that it was particularly important to:

"Open the door to our ***practice***." This met with general approval and shortly after another participant added, "It's not just open practice … its open ***minds***," implying that practitioners should be accepting of diverse opinions and even disagreement when offered in a respectful manner. Yet another participant said,

> It is more than open practice and open minds. … It's about open ***hearts*** too.

Their busy schedules had left little time to reflect on their practice, and on their place within their team, or time to support one another. Mutual care is crucial for staff morale. If colleagues lose faith in their practice, and feel isolated from others (as was often the case during Covid "lockdown"), emotional distance can become an accomplice to dehumanising processes.

When organisations become authoritarian in their implementation of directives and oversight of practice, practitioners become restricted in their creative endeavours and sometimes fearful that to challenge the rules risks losing their jobs. I often notice this damaging process when supervising experienced therapists who hold responsible roles within their organisations. A lack of creative connections between professionals leads to exhaustion and affects service delivery adversely. Moral courage to challenge can seep away if you are the lone voice of protest.

It is a reminder that, "If no one cares when someone takes the trouble to do things right, nothing changes and the overwhelming message to the people who work at the front line … is that no one notices excellence and no one cares. … That is the biggest source of burn out and discouragement for health care workers everywhere" (Gawande, 2014).

As the above anecdote suggests, not all constraints restrict possibilities for improved practice if the restrictions are addressed and altered. However, it would be naïve to write about creative practices without taking account of pressures and stresses upon service delivery. There is no short cut to good practice. It requires attention to the dimensions addressed in the Swedish anecdote: good supervision, manageable caseloads, open-hearted practice, and a system that recognises mutual learning, support, and the active contribution to service development by the children and families who use our services. Systemic practice is informed by critical self-reflection and critical reflection on the very organisations, policies and procedures that shape opportunities to work creatively.

Restrictions to creativity in practice can come from organisational demands that over-focus on bureaucratic "must do's," copious computer notes, too much time spent at a desk instead of seeing clients, risk-averse treatment models and overly stretched staff with heavy caseloads (see Wilson, 2017). The net effect of sustained pressure is not only the restriction of creativity in practice but also an impoverishment of services as staff decide to leave and further diminish the pool of expertise. The users of such services suffer. The Swedish training example describes the foundations of good co-creative practice, and you, dear reader, may be in sympathy and have experienced many of the stressors mentioned here. I cannot overestimate the need for supportive peer and management systems to uphold a level of critical, reflective thinking and co-practices that helps sustain staff in such busy organisations. To be playfully serious and creative in one's work life needs sustenance from various sources that I will return to in Chaps. 6 and 7.

For now, I wish to highlight the importance of maintaining a focus on wider socio-political forces in our practice, drawing attention to what Erich Fromm refers to as the forces that move or push us, as if from behind our backs (Fromm, 1981). Recognising and attending to these forces allows us the opportunity to act and to free ourselves from such limitations, including the way language can restrict options for creative possibilities.

Professional Language Can Restrict Options for Creativity

Diagnostic categories can be useful by reassuring a patient and providing clear pathways for appropriate treatment for many physical illnesses. But psychiatric diagnoses can be problematic, especially when children's expressions of distress are treated only as disorders to do with perceived individual pathology. The shorthand descriptions of a child as having a disorder (ADHD, ASD, OCD) are diagnoses that can trip off the tongue so easily that we can forget the impact of a "Disorder" on a child's identity and on all those in his life (Brady, 2005; Timimi, 2007, 2009). When a child is seen as having a disorder, conversation between the practitioner and the child's family can be dominated by discussion of medication, dosage and the child's behavioural responses to medication. This may be useful in some cases, but this is a very restricted realm of conversation that will obscure or ignore wider relational and contextual factors contributing to a child's perceived disorder (Wilson, 2015).

Aside: When I worked in a psychiatric service, I saw many children initially referred for treatment for ADHD. Once my systemic team and I began working with them and their families many of the children improved without recourse to medication. The point of entry into a service, and subsequent formulation of a child's problem, shapes the language of treatment and the form of therapy offered. Even when parents retained their view that their child still had ADHD, the language of diagnosis and pathology gradually faded from significance as other matters were addressed. A systemic approach invites a more relational frame for conversation for all participants.

One family talked with me of their eight-year-old son George's ADHD behaviour becoming increasingly problematic after his younger brother was hospitalised. The parents explained that George had thought he had caused his brother's serious illness, at which point the ADHD got worse. Through a careful exploration of the child's feelings of guilt, and with reassurance from his parents, George's guilt and ADHD symptoms lessened.

The power of a diagnosis can become less confining in situations where contextual and relationally focused discussions are permitted and fresh perspectives on a child's problematic behaviours are explored. To directly challenge the parent's view that George had ADHD would have been an error. What engaged their curiosity was a sensitive shift in focus towards the child's worry about causing his brother's illness. George continued to be a "busy boy" but less was made of ADHD as a cause and George did not require medication. Widening the lens of exploration drew the conversation away from seeing ADHD as a fixed state. Instead, George's behaviour was seen as an expression of his distress that was relationally situated. Emphasis on medication, repeat prescriptions, parent training and behavioural management may be useful in some cases but stop other more creative discussions and options from being explored. The key is to help move the clients towards a sense of agency over the alleged symptom (Wilson, 2013).

Pause for Reflection

Before reading on I invite you to take some time to consider the following reflective exercise. To repeat my invitation at the beginning of the book, it is important to value those skills and abilities already in your practice repertoire. The aim is to add what works for you in developing your practice with children and families and also to think about taking some creative risks in moving out of your practice "Comfort Zone."

Circles of Opportunity and Constraint

Part One: Think for a few minutes on your current skills and abilities that aid you in your meetings with children and young people, both in your life outside your profession and inside your practice. Give yourself time to imagine how your young clients already appreciate these abilities in your practice repertoire. What are the features of your ways of working that enhance your connections with children?

Part Two: Now take a few minutes to draw a circle and write down inside the circle those skills you already possess. Next, draw a wider circle outside the first one. The distance between the two circumferences is the area open to your development usually associated with some risk, surprise, mistakes and anxiety but it is an area that one moves towards when adding to one's repertoire.

Take some minutes to write inside this larger circle those practices that could extend your current repertoire in a direction you feel you are able to take. These are realistic, step-wise moves that are within your reach. Itemise these and think of some children you meet already in your practice who would welcome your taking these new steps in your ways to connect with them and their problems.

Once you are satisfied with the plans for extending your reach, please draw a third circle outside the second one. In this wider circle place those steps that would create too much stress, too much risk or too much uncertainty for you. This is the area where one's development outreaches possibilities and makes practitioners fearful. The excitement of trying out something new gives way to a constriction often determined by structural/contextual forces that push us from behind our backs. These may be concerns about overloaded practice/lack of team support/bureaucratic pressures.

Finally, consider opportunities to develop fresh initiatives in your practice alongside other like-minded colleagues. Where are the resources not only within your own ways of working but within your team and your close allies? Look at what is possible to do not only on your own but alongside others who value your endeavours.

Therapeutic practice involves complex interactions between therapist, child and the network of relations within which a child lives. It is also impacted by the organisations within which practice is delivered, including the professional language used to describe and define a child's problems. In the next chapter I describe examples of a playfully serious systemic approach to bring the foregoing ideas into a more detailed description of the process of therapy over time. They illustrate my practice at a busy Child and Adolescent Mental Health service in London where I worked as a consultant systemic therapist and member of a multidisciplinary team.

References

Andersen, T. (Ed.). (1990). *The reflecting team*. Norton.

Brady, G. (2005). ADHD, diagnosis, and identity. In C. Newnes & N. Radcliffe (Eds.), *Making and breaking children's lives*. PCCS Books.

Cecchin, G. (1987). Hypothesising circularity and neutrality revisited: An invitation to curiosity. *Family Process, 26*, 405–413.

Cecchin, G., Lane, G., & Ray, W. (1992). *Irreverence: A strategy for therapists' survival*. Karnac Books.

Cecchin, G., Lane, G., & Ray, W. (1994). *The cybernetics of prejudices in the practice of psychotherapy*. Karnac.

Dallos, R., & Draper, R. (2010). *An introduction to family therapy: Systemic theory and practice*. Open University Press.

Fromm, E. (1981). *On disobedience. Why freedom means saying "no" to power*. Harper Perennial.

Gawande, A. (2014). Reith lecture: The idea of wellbeing. *BBC Broadcast*, 20 December 2014.

Palazzoli, M., Boscolo, L., Cecchin, G., & Prata, G. (1978). *Paradox and counter-paradox*. Jason Aronson.

Palazzoli, M., Boscolo, L., Cecchin, G., & Prata, G. (1980a). Hypothesising, circularity, neutrality: Three guidelines for the conductor of the interview. *Family Process, 19*(1), 3–11.

Palazzoli, M., Boscolo, L., Cecchin, G., & Prata, G. (1980b). The problem of the referring person. *Journal of Marital and Family Therapy, 6*, 3–9.

Schon, D. A. (1986). *The reflective practitioner: How professionals think in action*. Basic Books.

Shotter, J. (2016). *Speaking, actually: Towards a new fluid common-sense understanding of relational becomings*. Everything is Connected Press.

Stith, S., Rosens, K. H., McCollum, E. E., Coleman, J. U., & Herman, S. A. (1996). *Journal of Marital and Family Therapy, 22*, 69–86.

Timimi, S. (2007). *Mis-understanding ADHD: The complete guide for parents to alternatives to drugs*. Author House.

Timimi, S. (2009). *Straight talking introduction to children's mental health problems*. PCCS Books.

White, M. (2011). *Narrative practice: Continuing the conversation* (D. Denborough, Ed.). Norton.

White, M., & Epston, M. (1990). *Narrative means to therapeutic ends*. W.W. Norton.

Wilson, J. (1998). *Child focused practice: A collaborative systemic approach*. Karnac.
Wilson, J. (2003). *Kindorientierte Therapie: Ein systemisch-kooperativer Ansatz*. Carl-Auer-Systeme Verlag.
Wilson, J. (2007). *The performance of practice: Enhancing the repertoire of therapy with children and families*. Karnac.
Wilson, J. (2013). A social relational critique of the biomedical definition and treatment of ADHD: Ethical, practical and political implications. *Journal of Family Therapy, 36*, 6–19.
Wilson, J. (2015). Family therapy as a process of humanisation: The contribution and creativity of dialogism. *Australian and New Zealand Journal of Family Therapy, 36*(1), 6–19.
Wilson, J. (2016). Engaging children and young people; A theatre of possibilities. In *Narrative therapies with children and their families* (A practitioner's guide to concepts and approaches) (2nd ed., pp. 91–111). Routledge.
Wilson, J. (2017). *Creativity in times of constraint: A practitioner's companion in mental health and social care*. Routledge.
Wilson, J. (2021). Boxed in?: Commentary on widening the screen: Playful responses to challenges in online therapy with children and families. *Journal of Family Therapy, 43*(2), 346–350.

5

Building Creative Relationships with Children: Four Case Illustrations in Detail—Practice and the Practitioner

All illustrations provide reflective commentary on learning points.

> From a removed perspective, you can divide [an experience] … into separate components, affects, cognitions, and a sequence of actions, perceptions as well as sensations. Each can be looked at separately. But first-person experience is not broken up like that; it is felt as a whole. (Stern, 2004, p. 35)

Therapeutic practice is a complex multi-sensorial engagement over time, and any description of practice is, unavoidably, an after-the-event account. Nevertheless, I have tried to capture the "in the moment" experiences that seemed particularly relevant as well as the wider holistic influences that were key components of my practice. These significant moments and wider influences acted as guides in finding useful fresh directions in meeting the young people and family members described in the following illustrations.

The first case focuses mostly on direct work with a teenage girl, the second on the family of a depressed fifteen-year-old boy. The third and fourth cases illustrate a wider focus to include the network of relationships surrounding the child or children involved.

J. Wilson, *Building Creative Therapeutic Relationships with Children and Young People*, Palgrave Texts in Counselling and Psychotherapy,
https://doi.org/10.1007/978-3-031-85706-5_5

Yasmin and Her Mother Nadia

Yasmin is a fourteen-year-old girl who lives with her mother and older brother. They are a Muslim family living in our catchment area in south-east London. Yasmin has been referred to our community psychiatric service because she is depressed and anxious, withdrawn and struggling in school.

It has been a busy morning, but I try to take a few minutes to focus on how to approach this mother and child who are likely to be anxious about coming to our service for the first time. The doctor's letter also states that Yasmin tried to swallow some poison (cleaning liquid) when she was nine years old and was referred to a service like ours at that time.

I am almost always a little nervous before meeting a new family, but I consider this feeling helps me to stay alert to how best to set them at ease, including my decision not to carry out a series of prescribed standard questions on meeting new clients until after I have met with the family.

Aside: When the first meeting with a family is geared towards completing standard questionnaires it can make family members uneasy. Some families may feel reassured by a set of standard questions at the outset but it is also likely that clients will feel the practitioner is more interested in completing the questionnaire than firstly making a human connection with them.

I enter the waiting room and am immediately struck by the stillness and silence in the room. The mother Nadia looks up at me with a slightly apprehensive expression and tries to smile. Yasmin sits beside her, very still, shrouded in a "hoodie," and keeps her eyes on the floor.

I find myself talking quietly; my voice is low, and I move slowly, nod and say hello but do not offer my usual handshake. Somehow that move would feel too intimate, too intrusive. I am standing apart from them and notice that Yasmin has taken a soft toy from the toy box in the waiting room. It is a tortoise, and she is holding this carefully in her lap. I introduce myself and ask if they would care to come to my room to meet. Yasmin looks up for the first time and I nod, glancing in her direction.

"*I see you have found a soft animal,*" I venture. … She nods. "*Please, if you'd like to bring this with you to my room that would be fine,*" I say, in a slightly lighter tone, easing gently into the cautious atmosphere, and already I sense a hint of some relaxation in my body. We quietly proceed to my room.

Reflections on my initial attempt to connect: I needed to find a manner of emotional and physical distance from Yasmin and Nadia that was not intrusive yet encouraged a respectful connection with both of them. This was more a matter of sensing the emotional atmosphere in the first moments of meeting them.

We improvise responses to another when we take care to notice their responses to us. In therapeutic practice we have a responsibility to try to create an atmosphere in which our clients feel respected and safe enough in our presence. Our sensorial responses help to gauge the appropriate "dance of intimacy" required in figuring out how best to create a safe enough context in which to meet.

Each behaviour is part of this dance of appropriate intimacy. With Nadia and Yasmin, the invitation was to go very slowly, quietly and at an emotional distance that neither felt intrusive nor too distant. Here was I entering the room. I am a tall white Scottish man, and I am standing above two people of colour, a woman of perhaps forty years and her diminutive daughter of fourteen. It is tempting to think that we, the professionals, are the only ones making an "assessment" of a situation when we meet with our clients. At the same time our new clients are also assessing us. What did the mother and daughter make of me? Their experiences of life will equally harbour ideas and prejudices about the other, so we are in effect involved in a process of mutual assessment, mutual search for connection that accommodates the differences between us.

Why did I focus on this small interaction between a child and a toy? The girl had picked the toy from the young children's toy box. Perhaps she was taking some comfort from the soft toy, like a younger child might do? I noticed that she stroked it several times as I was introducing myself. We notice more than we have permission to comment on at the moment of noticing but store our observations for later.

As the Session Progressed

The conversation with Nadia and Yasmin slowly unfurled to invite each of them to help me gain an appreciation of their concerns. I needed to ascertain their wishes and expectations from our service. Throughout this session the pace was slow and tentative with Nadia doing most of the talking and, occasionally, Yasmin nodding in agreement about her feeling "*worried about things.*" At one point I took a small risk: "*Yasmin … that tortoise you have been looking after, it doesn't have a name. I wonder if by the end of our first meeting you could come up with a name for it?*" At this she looked interested, less hidden in the hoodie and a little more relaxed in her movements.

Although Yasmin was quiet, I began to feel that she did not want to give up on the possibility that we might, somehow, become of help to her. I was certainly more at ease now in the session. As I was about to suggest another meeting, I asked Yasmin if she had managed to give the tortoise a name, at which point she said, "*She is called Amaryllis.*" I replied, "*What a beautiful name! Could you do me a favour? Amaryllis is not too happy being kept in a box. Would you mind taking her home and bringing her with you to our next meeting?*" Yasmin liked this idea and so the initial meeting ended on a much lighter note than it had begun.

Later Reflections on What Contributed to Making a Useful Connection With Yasmin and Nadia

Yasmin and I had begun to create a form of imaginative play. She entertained the idea that a toy could be unhappy at spending time in a box! She accepted my invitation for her to care for the toy and to give it a name. This form of playful exchange is **NOT** the precursor to doing the **REAL** therapy; it is the first move in the beginning of a dialogue with the child and her mother. I enter into the exchanges with Yasmin without too much direction except to try to set her a little more at ease. I could speculate that perhaps my talk of caring for the tortoise was a metaphor denoting the invitation by me to "look after" the therapy that may develop. The girl's caressing of the tortoise, a creature that likes to hide inside its shell, just as Yasmin hid inside her heavy clothing, was a connection I only made after the session. Sometimes we simply respond as a hunch, a guess, in a fleeting moment, hoping that something useful may transpire. These reflections were not fully formed in the instant of meeting the girl and her mother; rather they became clearer after the event and helped to shape my subsequent work with them.

John Shotter (2016) describes this acting in the moment as an expression of "spontaneous responsiveness," a readiness to respond in accord with another when one is immersed in the here-and-now experience of meeting.

General Learning Points

Motivation Is Co-created

Motivation to work together is jointly created, and with Yasmin and her mother the sessions began to take shape, first by establishing a mutually respectful relationship with both clients in which they began to see me as competent. In turn I became aware of their strengths and growing commitment to our sessions. The agreed direction of the therapy bound us in a joint commitment which was to help Yasmin return from depression and feeling anxious most of the time. The flickers of this joint endeavour began with her looking after of the soft toy, Amaryllis. Nadia in the meantime hoped I would take care of her daughter and in part wished to hand this responsibility over to me so it was important to keep Nadia involved in reviews of any progress Yasmin and I made.

Progress Is Not a Lineal Process

Sometimes progress seems straightforward but most often therapy stumbles and trips up so that the direction of travel is not always clear. Good, effective practice does not often take place in miracle moments of revelation. It more commonly occurs through incremental, often complicated, sometimes unclear, ideas or chance occurrences about how to proceed.

However, persistence, realistic optimism, consistency and a willingness to remain present, to be available when crises arise, are the features that children and families describe as important when asked about what helped them in therapy. Our practice depends on a mutual learning process of trial and error, reflection, renegotiation and experimentation, and is fundamentally a process of humanisation. Turning points are indicators of progress.

Note Special Turning Points, Unfolding the Unsaid

The next two sessions took place weekly, and we jointly decided that I should meet with Yasmin on her own for a few sessions with feedback to Nadia, jointly agreed with Yasmin.

After a few sessions in which we seemed to be on safer ground, Yasmin came to her next session looking more intense than before as if she had something on her mind. We began by catching up on school, her friendships and how she was feeling. The atmosphere was expectant.

Aside: Sometimes I find myself working too hard to engage in conversation with a young client and if I recognise this happening I deliberately slow down to leave space for silence between the spoken words.

Yasmin begins to tell me that she once lived with her mother and Aunt Monica. The aunt was disabled, and Yasmin's mother was given the role of carer of the aunt. As she begins to tell me about life with her aunt she hesitates. … I wait. … and then she recounts her story of being beaten by her aunt and how nothing was done to stop this. At this moment I am anxious not to interrupt her with questions about the details of the beatings but instead I remain attentive and still. Eventually Yasmin pauses and I ask her if she has ever talked about this before. She tells me that she has not done so and how it makes her very angry when she thinks about the beatings and the injustice.

I learn that the beatings happened several years ago, and Aunt Monica has since died. I ask Yasmin,

> *If you could tell your aunt how hurt and angry you are by the beatings what would you say to her?*

Yasmin shook her head, "*I could not say anything to her!*"

I mention that I have learned from other young people I have met that it can help to write to a person who has hurt them even if that person is not alive anymore.

> *Aside: It can be especially useful to share with children the wisdom of other children who have faced similar challenges in Life. This is a form of shared communal wisdom where the therapist is a conduit to pass on his learning from others. In addition, it is sometimes easier for children to reveal painful events to a cultural outsider. This can somehow diminish feelings of shame.*

Yasmin says, "*I couldn't write to Aunt Monica even though she is dead!*"

"*Ok,*" I say. "*I have an idea … how about if I could become your secretary and you are my boss. I can do the writing, and you can tell me what to put in the letter? How about that?*"

Yasmin looks pensive and cautiously agrees.

I sit at right angles to Yasmin, with a pen and paper ready to "take dictation."

Yasmin hesitates then begins to dictate very slowly the letter to the aunt. It takes shape over some minutes (excerpts below):

> *Dear Aunt Monica,*
>
> *I am glad you never had children because you don't deserve to be happy … . You beat me and did not say sorry. … The worst thing was when I had to wear winter clothes in the summertime….*

I paused here and asked Yasmin why she had to wear winter clothes in the summertime, and she replied in a clear voice that the winter clothes covered over her bruises.

I was moved by this childlike, candid explanation and felt tears in my eyes. I was taken aback by the image of a young girl covering her bruises when she went to school. Yasmin noticed my tears. I could only say, "*That's awful.*"

We eventually finished the letter. Yasmin asked me to keep it for her. When the letter was put aside Yasmin said, "*There is something else I have to tell you.*" I expected her to disclose some further abuse, but she said,"*I want to transgender.*" And so began the next stage of therapy.

The indication of her wish to change gender was the beginning of a lengthy process and deserves exploration in its own right. However, for the purposes of this text, I wish simply to emphasise the various elements within our attempts to create a safe context to generate fresh openings in therapeutic dialogue.

Reflections on This Session

We listen with every sense. In this illustration Yasmin engaged in a playful though serious reversal of roles in which I became her secretary to write the letter to Aunt Monica. It provided her with a safe enough context to begin to unfold the previously unspoken words about her unjust treatment. She played with me, and in this opening, she took the further courageous step to acknowledge the secret of her desire to change gender.

Children, like adults, will wait until they feel ready to talk with us about deeply held worries. It is as if the beginnings of the relationship have within them possibilities that only emerge when the time is right. Sometimes we must wait and allow ourselves to be surprised by what our clients reveal to us.

Postscript on Yasmin and Her Family: The Context Shapes Possibilities

This example aims to illustrate the micro moves, feelings and observations that helped to develop a useful connection with Yasmin. The practice later included her mother, a link with a transgender organisation that offered her ongoing support, and eventually a social care organisation that assisted her when leaving home. The wider context of her culture was a significant factor in shaping her future direction. Yasmin now wished to be called Raphael and be referred to as "he." Dealing with the complexity of how to ensure Rafael was safe from potential abuse involved other professionals, and discussions were held to help Rafael move into supported accommodation. The wishes of Raphael were uppermost in the minds of those professionals involved. It was important to acknowledge that Rafael's brother and separated father were both fundamentalist Muslims and Raphael's father had been radicalised when he returned to Pakistan. This created a deep concern for me and my colleagues, as to disclose Raphael's wishes to his father or older brother would likely put him at severe risk. Rafael was adamant that this should not happen, and his wishes were respected.

This is an example of how practitioners need to have both a detailed focus on the life of an individual and a wide-angle lens on the various contexts that can have a profound impact on what it is possible to achieve. The case example also illustrates the importance of co-operative multi-agency involvement. Complex psychosocial problems require clear dialogue and openly supportive social practices that embrace the wider contexts of a child's life and predicaments.

Some years after, I was contacted by Rafael who told me that he'd been successful in studying at college and was pleased with his career working in social media. At age eighteen he had decided to remain physiologically female.

In contrast to the emphasis on individual work with Yasmin/ Rafael, the following case illustration focuses on the important network around a young person who decided not to take part after my first session with him. His indirect involvement in the series of sessions is an example of a young person who was physically absent but always present in thinking about how to assist himself and his family.

The "Resistant" Patient

This is my first meeting with Jason, a fifteen-year-old boy referred to me as suffering from anxiety and depression. As with Rafael, I met Jason and Kelly his mother in the waiting room. Jason did not look at me. The silence was stony. I began by asking if both Jason and his mother would wish to meet with me and, after much hesitation, Jason nodded consent to meet, firstly on his own, and later with his mother.

Aside: The initial negotiation amongst family members and therapist is crucially important in preparing how to begin. The therapist must try to read the various persons' degrees of willingness or apprehension about taking part and the tolerable strain that family members may experience when coming to a therapy session together. ***The biggest error is when a family therapist insists that all family members must be present.*** *This can be felt as a massive imposition that can lead to families dropping out before any chance of therapeutic connection can be made. The point is not to impose a structure that does not fit. Rather, the therapist is aiming to make a useful connection with each person, validating their apprehension and reassuring them where there are uncertainties about the rationale for meeting together (as outlined in Chap. 3). The initial meeting is a negotiation to establish how to proceed and who should participate.*

A Surprising Start

I met Jason for the first and only time when he eventually came with me to my therapy room. On entering my room, he sat down and immediately began to sob, a heart-rending sob that perplexed me. I did not know what to say or do but something told me to wait and not interrupt his sobbing. At last, after what seemed like a long time, the boy's tears subsided, and his sighing ceased. During this time, I sat in silence with lowered eyes, a spontaneous gesture that seemed to reflect the profound sadness in the boy's tears. I noticed my own sighs in sympathy with Jason. When my breathing relaxed, I asked him if he would like to sit in silence for a while. He nodded and after some more moments I asked him if he would like his mother to join us and he again nodded his agreement.

Aside: Silence can be felt as reverential, promoting reflection, paying attention to words already spoken. Silence can also be experienced as oppressive, embarrassing or shameful. With Jason the silence between us was a movement that I was involved in, and conveyed to me just how desperately unhappy this young person felt. I felt a weight in my stomach and a wish to comfort him. Yet, instead, I needed to accept the tension and the desperate sadness without the temptation to try to ease his sadness with too much reassurance. To be present means to be in touch with another by not imposing on their experience.

:oming more confident in her dealings with Jason. She had begun to out socially again. She remarked that the journeys to our clinic had :n the first regular outings she had had for over a year.

Aside: Some of the strategies in the Think Tank sessions are similar to methods used in Non-Violent Resistance. See, for example, Jakob 2022.

In time Jason agreed to meet with a home tutoring teacher who also ended our Think Tank sessions, and the weekly sessions were stepped wn to fortnightly and then monthly as Jason continued to re-enter the rld of his peers, schooling and social life. The involvement with Jason's nily ended after about six months by mutual agreement.

Reflection: An important feature of systemic practice is to conceptu-se children's distress as an invitation, albeit a very painful and often lirect request to help them in their life. In this instance Jason made a y straightforward and direct statement to me at the outset that it was mother who needed the therapy. However, simply to change focus to Kelly as the patient would have been an error given Kelly's statement ıt she wanted help for her son, not herself.

Not having Jason present in therapy sessions made it difficult to justify case remaining open as the policy of the psychiatric service requires ıt a child must be physically present in treatment. Furthermore, if a ild refuses to attend appointments after two invitations, the case should closed.

This is an understandable response when staff resources are stretched yond their capacity, but it is a very limited perspective on how best to lp some so-called resistant clients and fails to appreciate that effective erapy can be achieved indirectly through recruiting significant people a child's life, even if the young person is not directly present in a ther-y session. Put simply, the systemic practitioner conceptualises the sys-n as the focus and treats the child in context.

Certainly, Jason was a sad and angry teenager and needed help but by using to participate directly in the sessions he prompted me and his nily to find other ways to be in touch with him. I used to send him itten updates after my sessions with his family in the belief that he ould appreciate my unstated acknowledgement of his wish for his

I invited Kelly, his anxious mother, to join us and w son she also began to cry and talked of her own deep sorr of her brother through suicide and her overwhelming gri her mother the year before. It was as if both mother ar onto their expressions of grief and desperation until they meeting.

At one point Kelly stopped the flow of her painful na rected herself by saying, "*But I'm not here to talk about m are here to help Jason!*"

As if fired into action by his mother's utterance, Jaso and shouted, "*It's not me that needs the fucking therapy .* promptly left the room. I did not see him again.

The dramatic exit left Kelly stunned, and me wonderi ceed. However, I was attentive to Jason's parting message t a challenge: Kelly wanted therapy for her son, and the mother to have therapy instead.

I asked Kelly to come the following week with Jason if not, she should come with members of her family who w about Jason. This led to weekly sessions with Kelly, her di John, and her twenty-year-old daughter Samantha. We m "Think Tank" sessions to discuss how to help Jason. Afte sent a written message to Jason to let him know he could s meetings if he wished.

Aside: It is not always necessary or helpful to define practice as in this case the idea of a series of "Think Tank" sessions was a construct that the family members found acceptable. It is imp with words to create a useful definition of family meetings: cons discussions/team talks/family gatherings are variations that can ing terms for some clients than "family therapy" sessions.

The sessions helped Jason's family to respond to him in tive ways: finding more de-escalating strategies to respon outbursts and demands on his mother, and searching for helpful friends of Jason to encourage him to leave his ro from time to time. As the sessions progressed Kelly

be go be at de w fa al in ve hi se th hi th cl b b h th in a te re fa w w mother to get help for herself. This was never overtly talked about but at the end of our six months of Think Tank sessions Kelly had become a much more outgoing, confident person whose own troubles were less dominant. She had found new horizons in mindfulness practices and sought a counsellor for herself.

The postscript to our work was a written card to me from Jason and his family in which he wrote, "*I am not anxious and depressed now. Thank you for helping my family.*"

Jason's words of thanks were unexpected but when one examines his message it is clear that he saw his depression as something that was treated by helping his family. It was a coded message that could read "Thank you for helping my mother."

However, I did not begin the Think Tank sessions with the strategic aim of directly helping Kelly. I focused on the resources within the family. These included debates about the best ways to respond to Jason's anger and sometimes omnipotent, controlling behaviour towards his mother. The sessions included devising strategies to respond more creatively to Jason and these were reviewed at each session. The practice held a relational focus that kept Jason central in our concerns. Although the practice with Jason and his family ended several years ago, it continues to inspire me because his family and eventually Jason showed a determination to expand their repertoires in thinking and behaving just as this book invites you, dear reader, to do.

The following example pays attention to negative feelings, failure, dismay and hopelessness, as these are also features of a therapist's experience and require acknowledgement. Often feelings of failure and errors in practice are left unexplored in texts and yet, from my experience as a trainer, I realise how important it is to own up to mistakes and failures. Students and fellow practitioners often appreciate that the so-called experts are not superhuman and the distance between beginner and experienced therapist is not a massive gulf that is beyond reach. What counts is our capacity to remain motivated and connected to what matters for the benefit of the clients concerned. In Chaps. 6 and 7 I focus on the intricacies of trying to move beyond impasses in therapy and feelings of hopelessness.

Three Boys and a Mother in Distress

This example illustrates the importance of feeling vulnerable and, at times, quite hopeless about progress in therapy with children. It is concerned with such fragile feelings of failure and the emotional impact on both the family and the therapist. Vulnerability and feelings of hopelessness are considered here significant and relevant emotions in the life of a therapist. Further, they can become initiators of constructive change when addressed sensitively.

Whilst working in a Child and Adolescent Mental Health Service I received three separate referrals on children from the same family.

Each child had his own file, and the expectation was that three separate assessments would be made on the three children. However, I decided to first meet with the family.

Rob, aged fifteen, was diagnosed as depressed and self-harming. He had recently injured his hand by punching a wall in the family home and on first meeting him I could see how defeated and desperate he was.

His younger brother Tom, aged ten, was receiving help in school because of his disruptive and aggressive behaviour towards other children in his class. In addition, the youngest child Simon, aged 7, was disabled and using a wheelchair following the sudden onset of an illness.

My first few meetings with the boys together with their mother made no progress. The parents were divorced and Jenny, the boys' mother, had sole care of her children. She had been receiving treatment for depression for some years and had relied on anti-depressants and little else to help her. She seemed resigned to helplessness and was worn out by the demands of her life. Resignation began to infect the relations between me and the family.

At the closure of the third session, I was concerned that, not only was my attempt to help failing to make progress, in fact the family's difficulties were increasing further. I decided to talk with them about my inability, so far, to be of help to them, and suggested that they might benefit from some form of respite care to relieve the stress they were under.

This suggestion was met with complete dismay. The feeling of hopelessness was pervasive. Jenny looked stunned by my suggestion and as they left the hospital, I saw how defeated they looked that I had taken away any last vestige of hope. It was the final session of the day, and I had a long journey home preoccupied with the defeated looks on their faces and downcast eyes as they walked away from me at the door of the clinic. My heart sank.

Self-Critical Reflections

When a Challenge Introduces Too Big/Too Little a Difference (After Tom Andersen personal communication)

I worried that my suggestion to think about respite care was too much of a challenge for them, only further contributing to their feelings of hopelessness. I thought they might drop out of the therapy. At the same time, I knew that "more of the same" family sessions would not help. I needed to somehow address the inert nature of our meetings so far. Not to do so would have been a therapeutic error.

We judge when to take a risk and live with a feeling of uncertainty (after Mason, 1993) and this judgement is based on one's sense of how a challenging statement may be received by the others in the conversation. The looks on the faces of the family members made me feel I had let them down. Sometimes when clients seem helpless the tendency is to work even harder, but this can often entrench the pattern. If one could give helplessness a voice it might say: "Please don't challenge me! I am too fragile to be challenged in any way. Please simply keep helping me to stay helpless!" A therapist should never challenge through the voice of indignation, anger or frustration. It must come from an appreciation of the context of helplessness, its logic, and a concern about the client's lives. This is more than an intellectual curiosity. It is based on care and concern, and this affective aspect of addressing helplessness is conveyed in the ways words are spoken. If I had said in an exasperated voice, "I THINK YOU REALLY NEED RESPITE CARE!" I am sure Jenny and her sons would have felt accused of their failures, further compounded by the critical tone of the therapist.

The Importance of Discussing Failure as a Way of Connecting

Without talking about our lack of progress the therapy would have become increasingly stagnant. The mention of respite care came from my feelings of not helping rather than an accusation that the family was to blame. This is a crucial distinction. I was concerned for their welfare, but I could not create any glimmer of hope, and the harder I worked the more I saw defeat in the responses from the family. My suggestion of respite care did not come from a deliberate strategic manoeuvre to mobilise the family's resources or a paradoxical injunction to make them resist my intervention. It was a statement to open the context to wider resources as my recent attempts to help had been ineffective.

The family returned, and to my relief and surprise, I entered a completely different atmosphere. Jenny sat upright. She looked much more present. She wanted to make the point that on no account was she giving in to the suggestion of respite care for her children.

Moving from 'Me/They' to 'We /Us'

What had happened? With hindsight I think my challenge had provoked the mother to fight for her sons and provide a much more creative effort that enabled us to begin to work together at last.

At one point I asked Jenny, "Who are the most important people involved in providing support for you and your sons?" There then followed a lively discussion on inviting all the professionals and Jenny's mother to a network meeting that Jenny and I would co-chair. She was to set the agenda as to what issues were uppermost in her mind and I would assist her in keeping the focus on her aims during the forthcoming meeting. This idea of communing a network meeting is not new to systemic practitioners but what is significant is the mother's commitment to engage in this process. My heart lifted. We had finally made an alliance and a joint focus. Dismay was replaced by a fresh sense of agency. This was a relational process between the family and me, not just a feature of the mother's new determination.

The following sessions were co-chaired by Jenny and me and led to useful meetings between those other professionals involved with the family in which Jenny set the agenda. This shift to a wider focus was possible because the failure to connect was addressed and acted to mobilise the mother's resources with the assistance of the co-chaired network meetings.

Tips on Therapist and Client Co-Chairing Sessions

It is crucial that the systemic therapist assists the client as co-chair. This means ensuring the focus is kept on a search for psychosocial resources by all members attending (Seikkula & Arnkil, 2014). This is a relational focus on possibilities, avoiding objectifying language, accusation or defensive posturing by any members attending. The hallmarks of systemic interviewing come into play: inviting opinions, interrupting redundant patterns, keeping curiosity and multiple perspectives in focus, and structuring conversation towards aims and themes uppermost in the interests of the client family. (This is a brief outline of the forms of questioning that such client-co-chaired sessions require.) In effect, the family therapist engages in the session as a coach to aid the client in holding a central position in the network meeting.

The client's agenda is pursued in a supportive, exploratory atmosphere of joint endeavour. It is not a formal case discussion, and it avoids any temptation to marginalise the client's voice, nor does it allow objectifying or objectionable language from participants.

Aside: Sometimes anxious colleagues may find it difficult to enter the more conversational and collaborative atmosphere of a co-chaired session and may resort to Case Conference mode describing clients in the third person, a form more suited to a courtroom than a co-chaired network meeting. Gentle encouragement is required to reorientate participants towards the collaborative atmosphere and purpose of the co-chaired session.

Amy and Her Terminal Illness

As a further illustration of this method I created a circumstance where Amy, the child patient, collaborated with me as a Co-Chair in an extended family network session.

The young girl, Amy, was referred to our Child and Adolescent Mental Health Service (CAMHS) as her family were in total disagreement about how to support Amy who had been diagnosed with terminal brain cancer. Amy was twelve years old. She came to CAMHS with her mother and Amy's express wish was for the arguments to end and for her large extended family to unite instead of remaining in such opposition. Many of the family arguments were linked to disagreements about how to deal with Amy's illness and its progression.

The co-chairing idea fitted Amy because she wanted her family to reunite and did not want her illness to remain a source of contention around who should support her and her mother.

It was clear from talking with Amy how important it was to her for the family feud to be resolved (before she died?). So, we met and discussed who should be invited to a family discussion (*note, not a therapy session*). Amy's mother helped to draw up a list of who to invite and, importantly, how the invitations were to be worded to best suit the relationship she had with each invited family member. I sent out the invitations, explaining my role having met with Amy. I explained in each letter that my job was to assist Amy in the discussion about her family and her concerns.

We booked the board room of the hospital, and all family members attended. Amy, small in stature, was proud to be at the head of the large board room table as Chair of the meeting. I sat near her and functioned as co-chair/facilitator as in the example above. It was an extremely moving event as Amy's terminal illness was discussed in ways that led to some partial resolution of family members' disagreements and negativity. It was the convening and structuring of this context that allowed a different conversation to occur, one in which the pain of addressing young Amy's illness was voiced. We followed her agenda as this was central to her concern and directly impacted her family.

Sometimes, as systemic therapists, we can help young children to voice that which is painful. We can offer words, not as prescriptions or interpretations, but as "good guesses," and invite their corrections or confirmation. Amy wanted to end a feud that, in her mind, was related to her diagnosis of terminal illness. It was as if this young girl wanted to "put her family's house in order" before she died. Amy's courage endures and still inspires me.

The co-chairing examples above are part of a wider orientation to systemic therapy that plays with the convention of the position of the therapist in the session. Co-chairing sessions place the therapist alongside the clients whilst still maintaining the role of therapist/coach/facilitator. Similarly, playing with the context of reflecting team work to invite family members to become reflecting teams/listening teams/joint team members with therapists is a variant of a method that democratises practice without jettisoning the therapist's contribution to help the setting for such experimentalist practices.

In all the above examples I have focused on the fine detail of practice. That is, the "in the moment," micro details of our experience when we meet clients in therapy. At the same time, I have hoped to illustrate the wide angle of a systemic perspective in searching for resources to help the child-in-context. Both dimensions of practice are equally important and mutually influential. The systemic, playfully serious practitioner sees the context of a child's life as the sphere within which co-creative possibilities will arise. Hope and realistic optimism are close allies of creativity.

References

Jakob, P. (2022). *Dem Trauma Widerstand Leisten: Neue Autoritat als familientherapeutischer und traumapadagogischer Ansatz*. Vandenhoeck & Ruprecht.

Mason, B. (1993). Towards positions of safe uncertainty. *Human Systems, 4*, 189–200.

Seikkula, J., & Arnkil, T. E. (2014). *Open dialogues and anticipations: Respecting otherness in the personal moment*. National Institute for Health and Welfare.

Shotter, J. (2016). *Speaking, actually: Towards a new fluid common-sense understanding of relational becomings*. Everything is Connected Press.

Stern, D. (2004). *The present moment in psychotherapy and everyday life*. W.W. Norton.

6

Part One: Embedded and Embodied Values—Part Two: Doing What Is Possible

Our actions express our values and our attitude towards the children and families we work with in our professional roles. But more than this, the values we try to uphold within our practice are not separated from the ways we see the world as a human being trying to weave our way through the complexities of life and the demands placed upon us. Certainly, we have a specific task to perform in our job as social worker or therapist but there is surely a base of values that shape our general orientation to one another inside and out with our professional activities.

The following is not a prescription for how to lead one's life but describes how my playfully serious attitude to my practice as a family therapist is built upon values and a political orientation that provides coherence to my orientation as a therapist with children and families. I invite you, dear reader, to consider where you stand on these matters. Chapter 7 also offers further ideas in providing a working philosophy of systemic practice, one that underpins my general approach as a systemic therapist.

J. Wilson, *Building Creative Therapeutic Relationships with Children and Young People*, Palgrave Texts in Counselling and Psychotherapy,
https://doi.org/10.1007/978-3-031-85706-5_6

Part One: Embedded and Embodied Values

The "Expert" in the Emperor's New Clothes (with Apologies to Hans Christian Andersen)

Some years ago, I took part in a conference comparing various approaches to strategic, brief, and systemic therapy. I was part of an "expert" panel asked to describe my systemic practice alongside three other presenters. One of the presenters was clearly imbued with his own position as "expert" and he demonstrated this attitude in his dismissive responses to any critical questions from the audience. I was sitting next to him becoming increasingly uncomfortable as he proceeded to present himself as entirely certain about the effectiveness of his work and expertise. Listening to all this, I felt slightly embarrassed on his behalf!

The "expert" then showed a video tape of his interview with a young woman who he patronised and constantly interrupted, whilst sitting on a higher chair than his patient. None of this seemed to bother the young woman who had been told the therapist was an expert in his field. She succumbed to his approach and clearly thought that his behaviour was acceptable. She was compliant and unquestioning. I do not know the outcome of his therapy with her, but I know it was an expensive private service he offered.

As I watched and listened, I heard the "expert" make all manner of pronouncements about what he was doing and what the effect would be on his patient. However, I could see no evidence of his claims and I was wondering what to say when a member of the audience called out, "You are talking bullshit!' and proceeded to dismantle the "expert's" pronouncements. The challenge led to a vociferous exchange between the "expert" and the challenging conference participant.

It struck me then, as it does now, that my approach is diametrically opposed to this version of a relationship between patient and therapist. This is a judgement based on values on how to treat one another as human beings whether or not we are therapists.

The writings of Paulo Freire have provided me with a backbone of ideas that help sustain me in my practice, and below I illustrate these briefly to give a summary of how Freire's ideas have helped shape my practice with children and families, illustrated in the foregoing chapters. In addition, the following chapter provides further reference to my practice philosophy as a form of radical systemic humanism.

The experience of witnessing the "expert" present his work sits in sharp contrast to the ways I try to meet with clients, students and supervisees. This does not make me pious or overly humble. I retain a critical, reflective capacity, and I am happy to share my opinions and expertise when I think this will be useful and responded to with curiosity or a step towards a more creative conversation. But The "Expert" in the Emperor's New Clothes illustration points out two important themes.

Firstly, that personal hubris is a real constraint to connection with others, especially those who occupy the position of a patient and are, to a degree, dependant on your treatment of them as another human being.

Secondly, powerful non-collaborative approaches may lead to compliant, passively dependant patients, and this is a dangerous position that dehumanises the patient and diminishes the humanity of the hubris-laden therapist.

Magical Consciousness

Let us return to the female patient in the Emperor's New Clothes anecdote. According to Freire, magical consciousness is a form of domesticated thinking that leaves the individual compliant within the status quo One might consider the young woman to be in this way "domesticated," dependant on the instructions from her therapist who holds the truth about how to proceed.

For Freire, dialogue and critical curiosity are central to ways human beings continue in a process of mutual humanisation. This position is critiqued by Fazzolari (2022), who argues that Freire's emphasis on dialogue and the continual process of developing complex dialogical relations results in "an emphasis on idealist and cultural transformations … without the finite objective,material, and structural revolution" (p. 62). However, for the systemic therapist, Freire's ideas focus attention on the immediacy of relationship as central to transformation. Educational development, and I propose, therapeutic development, occurs within a process of conscientisation whereby human beings become aware of and act upon those matters that oppress them. Oppressive forces external to the individual become, in Freire's terms, internalised. In drawing parallels with systemic practice, we become alerted to the micro details of interaction that act to oppress (insults, threatening looks, passive acceptance and so on) as well as the macro political and structural contexts that impact each of us (poverty, racism classism, climate change and political unrest). The therapist places emphasis on both the micro and macro influences that constitute the complex context of meeting with a family or individual in therapy. Creating a generative conversation attentive to wider socio-political impacts on clients' lives is useful when a connection is made between the immediate lived experience of the client's family AND the socio-political and cultural impacts on their lives. In this way the conversation remains rooted to the client's central concerns. It is not a lecture on experiences of social oppression more suited to a sociology lecture.

It is a matter of timing and sensitivity to introduce fresh perspectives when they are likely to be received with a degree of interest. Otherwise, we impose our ideas on the other without invitation. This is a delicate matter as sometimes, as in the case example above with the mother and her sons, I introduced a challenge that upset the clients yet ultimately led to a more positive direction in the therapy. So, challenge and debate are part of the systemic therapist's repertoire but this needs to be done whilst holding firm to the ideas of mutual humanisation.

Following Freire, a person should not become a "prisoner of a 'circle of certainty' within which reality is also imprisoned. On the contrary, the more radical the person is, the more fully he or she enters into reality so that, knowing it better, he or she can better transform it. … This person is not afraid to enter into dialogue" (Freire, 1996, p. 21).

For therapists to avoid falling prey to circles of certainty it is necessary to critically address our professional organisations, professional affiliations and particularly the conditions under which we work. Do you see yourself increasingly providing a service that lacks commitment or that contradicts what you believe in? These are questions practitioners deal with and need, somehow, to address. In a recent workshop in Denmark, I spent three days with highly committed social work colleagues all affiliated with the field of adults' and children's mental health. Many were dedicated to doing a thoroughly professional job of caring for their clients (or citizens as they called them). In conversation and in workshop exercises it became apparent that many of them were extremely tired and worn down by bureaucracy and too many demands on their time and energy. Some of these challenges to creativity have already been addressed in foregoing chapters but the question remains how one takes action to counter those practices and organisational features that would limit creativity and effective practice and threaten to dehumanise client and practitioner.

Gawande (2014) emphasises the importance of care, consistency, conscientiousness and commitment in any practice of worth. These four qualities ring true as baselines for creativity in building bridges with children and families often revealed in the minute details of our interaction with the families seeking our help. They are also qualities to value in our relationships with colleagues and team members.

Professional Language Can Distance as Well as Create Connection

I have written elsewhere (Wilson, 1998, 2015, 2017) of the potential damage that lies in objectifying clients by restricting their identity to a diagnostic category. Whilst an accurate diagnosis can be extremely useful in finding pathways to treatment, this should not stop the systemic therapist from connecting with the person as a whole.

When mental health and social care services are stretched and bound by diagnostic categories, it is not surprising that acronyms are employed to describe a client or shorthand descriptions are made of a child's or adults' difficulties. It helps to frame direction for treatment, but it risks overemphasising the diagnosis instead of searching for connections beyond the identified problem behaviour. One of the thrusts towards building bridges with children and their families is a search for psychosocial resources whilst also respecting the "problem talk" that is usually on the lips of the family members' initial contact with a therapist. This means listening to the words of concern, problem definition and attempted solutions, BUT the conversation does not go down the rabbit hole of being lost in pathology. Instead, the therapist looks for the potentiality in the family and a co-created route to new directions.

In a recent online workshop I offered, I was dismayed when a young therapist risked being disciplined by her manager for using the word "genocide" in a family meeting with refugees from Gaza. This sanction was placed upon her, despite the family members' use of the term during the therapy session to describe their experience of the war. The language was deemed too biased, inaccurate, and was therefore struck out of the conversation. The therapist felt unsafe, unable to be free in her therapeutic discussion with family members for fear of saying "the wrong word." When a therapeutic context is constrained by a fear of opening dialogue in matters that are profoundly important, the censorship of words becomes a censorship of creative possibilities. Here the politics of practice sears itself right into the micro interactions of a family session and between the therapist and the overseeing management.

Freedom of expression needs of course to be monitored so that the therapist is mindful of the impact of her language, her whole presence, upon the children and families she meets. But there should be room for experimentation, for moving beyond strict protocols and, as argued in the foregoing pages, a sense of improvisation. To feel free to enter these resourceful domains requires a safe enough context as described earlier in Chap. 3. We should also be mindful that the language, methods and general orientation of a therapist can influence the meanings clients give to the matters being discussed. Our clients can begin to learn the language and style of our therapeutic approach as we develop a form of collaborative meaning making.

Gianfranco Cecchin of the Milan Associates joked with me that he could often tell the type of therapy and even the name of the therapist who had met with his new client simply by the ways the client couched the description of their predicament in language derived from the previous therapist's manner and lexicon!

On a more serious note, Bruce Wampold (2001) makes the point that one of the key features of a successful outcome in therapy is the client's belief that the therapy will work. Without confidence in the ability of the therapist and, I would argue, the human caring curiosity of the therapist, the necessary conditions for creative conversations will be limited. Our clients can begin to learn the language and style of our therapeutic approach as we develop a form of collaborative meaning making, and this places a responsibility on all practitioners to be careful in their use of words, their demeanour and their sense of hospitality towards those who seek our help.

When Co-creativity Is Not on the Horizon: What Then?

In so many of the case examples I have used to illustrate my practice there has been a shift from caution, reluctance and nervous anticipation met by my attempts to create a safe enough respectful context to continue. Yet, many practitioners and therapists work within a remit of statutory involvement with clients where a third party is either directly or indirectly involved, such as in high-conflict divorce proceedings or statutory childcare interventions where the legal system has oversight of practice. In my experience as a social worker and consultant to colleagues in such interventionist services, the same principles of caring curiosity must prevail. This is a difficult position to maintain when conflict and adversity is prevalent in the relationships with clients and there is no foothold for a collaborative connection with members of a family. Here the therapist/practitioner needs to be on guard to avoid being swept up in the dynamics of conflict and reactivity so common in highly conflictual cases.

Good supervision is necessary to try to maintain an attitude of compassion when this is in short supply. But it is also important to recognise that our strong feelings of anger, dislike or profound sadness are natural and cannot be erased by technique. This acknowledgement makes our encounters once again a human experience, not a technical or scientific experiment.

Systemic training helps the practitioner to entertain multiple views and seriously consider the various perspectives present whilst also being able to make a professional judgement that privileges one perspective over others. Childcare practices are fraught with concerns of this nature: deciding what action to take when a child is at risk of physical and/or emotional abuse, when to work with a couple where domestic violence has been part of the history of their relationship, or when continuing high-conflict divorce cases create severe emotional abuse for the children involved.

These matters highlight the therapist's ethical and statutory contexts of practice where a collaborative co-creative approach is not immediately feasible. It requires the ability to distinguish between a potential or actual therapeutic contract and the impossibility of such a procedure. Without this critical distinction one might persist with a pseudo-therapeutic (non-)alliance to the detriment of the people involved, and in high-risk situations this is a dangerous position to take.

Can a humanising co-creative process prevail within the relational complexity of statutory and interventionist contexts for practice? I believe so. There are some caveats, however: To treat another as a human being with consideration, respect and dignity does not exclude taking a statutory action that runs contrary to their wishes. As a social worker, I recall meeting with clients who despised social work intervention and my role with them. They hated the oversight and supervision I provided especially in matters of child neglect. At the same time, my belief was that these oppositional clients should be treated with sensitivity and in so doing I and my team colleagues refused to objectify those who despised our involvement in their lives. This is not a pious position. Of course, there were times when social workers "let off steam" to colleagues but this was our way of clearing the ground to return to our practice without frustrations spilling over into the direct work with the oppositional clients. In this emotionally complex arena of practice, the playfully serious practitioner keeps the door open on any potentially therapeutic connection without being naïve! In doing so the client experiences a new response, one that does not objectify them, or lead to anticipated emotional escalations.

Section Two: Becoming a Possibilist

Throughout my practice and teaching over my career I have learned to become a Possibilist (Wilson, 2011), that is, neither a pessimist nor a naïve optimist. One trap for therapists is an overweening belief that the model they espouse will create remarkable changes in people's lives, and some even believe that a pure application of a model will yield even better outcomes. This is what I mean by false or naïve optimism. On the other hand, some practitioners have their sights set too low and fail to see the potential in any encounter to create something positive. If therapists lose heart, become cynical or lose faith in their approach this signals a disillusionment that is detrimental to service delivery and requires urgent attention.

Adopting a Possibilist orientation is an option in situations where one feels that persistence will eventually be rewarded by opening up fresh therapeutic directions. This is in contrast to an overly headstrong persistence which does not acknowledge the lack of any engagement from the clients. Working hard to find a useful connection with a family should not be at the cost of the therapist doing all the work while the family become passive participants in the therapist's hard work and good intentions. At each step in the relational dance the Possibilist therapist considers how to move in response to the responses from the client or family.

Creating Possibilities in Finding Connections

In the following section I return to a focus upon the moment-to-moment moves or "dance steps" that we make when we try to build creative bridges with young clients and families. In earlier chapters I described specific practice examples in detail. Here I focus on a series of steps for you to consider. I have coupled them together to make it easier to describe their contrasting features. In practice the complexity of our engagement with our clients means we are always moving in response to what is offered by them and what we think could help create a useful therapeutic direction. This, as argued in the detailed case examples, is a form of improvisation informed by a systemic theoretical orientation.

> Change is based on lived experience. In and of itself verbally understanding, explaining, or narrating something is not sufficient to bring about change. ... An event must be lived with feelings and actions taking place in real time, in the real world, with real people, in a moment of presentness. (Stern, 2004)

This quote from Stern can appear daunting to many practitioners in search of "what to do" in practice. As a beginning family therapist, I recall the fear I experienced in sitting in front of an expectant family in therapy and wondering how I would conduct the session. I needed a plan, a campaign, techniques to know how and what to ask, how to balance the session by ensuring many voices were heard. This scaffolding helped me build a conversation that had purpose and direction. Above all, I needed to look as if I knew what I was doing even if I felt rudderless in the sea of words emerging in the session.

It is important for me to recall these early days as it can seem too easy to marginalise the importance of planning a session beforehand, particularly if one is just beginning to immerse oneself in the world of systemic praxis. The importance of planning and preparation for a family session has been discussed earlier. The focus in this section is on the complex interactions between therapist and family that cannot be fully planned ahead of time. In this section I address the importance of moving "in a moment of presentness" as described by Stern. Although these movements cannot be pinned down, the various pairings I offer suggest a schema for you to consider. The pairings offer a chance to reflect on your ways of responding in each unique encounter with your clients and improve the range of ways to connect with them.

Not Dancing in the Dark

Since each of us has our unique style as a practitioner these steps are not intended as marching orders, more a waltz, quickstep or tango, depending on your own ways of moving when you meet with your clients. In reading the following "dance steps" it is important to consider the steps as a part of a relational dance, not a separate manoeuvre.

Further, the family therapist must attempt to be in step with several people at the same time in the same encounter, so the steps can become even more important to focus upon. At any one time a therapist may be observing one family member looking wary, another looking disinterested, or a child seeking comfort.

The skill of the systemic therapist is in noticing all these complex responses and judging how and when to connect with each person

present. This relational "dance" of words, actions and feelings involves a number of participants and calls upon the therapist to be a choreographer for the session at one point and "dance" partner at another moment.

Tip: Learn to notice the small steps of curiosity

I offer a short illustration here to emphasise the benefit of therapists noticing small movements not immediately addressed. The timing of our questions and statements, and observations, should be based on when we anticipate our words may be heard with interest. Sometimes we notice more than we can immediately address openly.

Picture the scene: I am meeting a family for the first time. The two parents are describing the troubles they are having with their ten-year-old son Tom. He is lying across a chair in the therapy room. His older brother and sister are in their teens, and they look interested in my initial welcoming comments.

Ten-year-old Tom doesn't look at all interested, but as the session proceeds I notice that he is becoming a little more curious about the opinions of his siblings and his parents. He begins to look up. In all the busy conversation with family members I notice, out the side of my eye, these small moves being made by the boy. I judge that to focus attention on him would be premature. I sense he might close off. I am particularly interested in Tom's attempts to disguise his interest in what others are saying and I consider that to continue hearing the views of his family members is beginning to intrigue him. Now all this is speculation on my part, but it is important to appreciate that family therapy interviews are unusual contexts for conversation. To have a facilitator conduct a family discussion can be an unusual experience and I reckoned that Tom was somehow enticed by my questions and invitations to hear the views of each family member. I thought it was likely that Tom would soon wish to contribute so I waited. This fragment from a session hints at the therapist's fine tuning to judge when to engage with those whose presence in a session appears marginal. I continued listening to others' views as to their concerns and worries about Tom. At a certain moment Tom becomes more animated and begins to join in the conversation.

Each "dance" step in our engagement with clients is part of a wider context, and hence we are always, to an extent, dancing in the dark when we meet with our clients. We cannot prejudge how our words and actions will be heard but we can anticipate a possible response. We sense some flickering possibility and dare to provoke this into conversation as with young Tom in the illustration here and in parts of the foregoing case examples outlined in Chap. 5.

We each have a range of responses when meeting another person but probably have a preferred default position, one that is employed naturally by us in social situations: welcoming, friendly, optimistic, curious, wary, reserved and so on But as therapists, we are also concerned to create a fit that will help make a safe enough connection with the others we meet in family therapy. This requires a degree of flexibility to find a connection that will allow a safe enough degree of emotional connection with each family member to ease the conversation in mutually productive directions. This is part of the art of connectionist approaches to practice (after Hoffman, 2002). It does not mean abandoning one's usual range of interactional skills but it does require a conscious use of aspects of one's repertoire in meeting with others that can be expanded and continually developed in response to the unique features of the people we meet in practice. The following are some important pairings of ranges of responses that a therapist can endorse as part of their relational skill development. It involves a degree of improvisation, where the therapist offers an "invitation" to a client and notices the response. He asks himself, in the moment, "Did this connect or did I manage to intrude too much with my observation." This toing and froing contributes to the life of a therapy session, and the following positional pairings are one way of addressing the range of possible responses that can help broaden one's repertoire.

Relational Attunement: Three Relational "Dances" to Consider

1. Emotional Connection: Closeness and Distance

We sense when another person moves too close to us in a social situation. It feels uncomfortable and our response is to step back. We judge when there is an appropriate non-intrusive distance between us and step forward or back to signal the degree of intimacy appropriate in each encounter with another. In therapy practice these are the physical and emotional steps we negotiate each time we meet with a client or family.

This aim becomes more complicated when we meet with several persons simultaneously. Here the therapist needs to be able to move, physically and emotionally, to attune with each contributor in a session. I recall observing a very skilful colleague create a warm engaging connection with a child in a family session only to receive critical looks from both parents. Here the therapist had moved towards an emotionally proximal stance with the child but failed to take account of the parents' reactions. So, while warmth and friendliness may be a generally useful way with many families it does not fit every situation. In the above scenario the therapist's friendly default position failed to impress the parents with their more distant and sceptical view of her attempt to engage their child.

I have made the same error from time to time in misjudging a child's reaction to my more open, inviting manner. One wary adolescent boy said to me, "Are you trying to be my friend?" His tone suggested he did not trust my friendly opening invitation. His message was a salutary one and required from me an explanation to the effect that my aim was to invite people to contribute to the session but not to feel in any way unsafe. I guessed from his response that he was not ready to make any open connection with a therapist and I needed to respect his statement.

Sometimes the reverse step is necessary. When children are brought to a therapist, they may have little or no idea what to expect, and as mentioned earlier in Chap. 3, it is important for the therapist to offer an age-appropriate explanation as to the purpose of the therapy and its aims. However, even when these ground rules are in place a therapist can make an error in assuming a young person will wish to contribute. Here the better option is to allow, even encourage, the young person to refrain from contributing. As described in the detailed examples with Yasmin and Jason, judging emotional closeness and appropriate distance was important is feeling my way into the permitted intimacy of the early connections with the children. Once a feeling of safe enough intimacy is established, it does not remain a fixed state but will alter in the course of the relationship with the young person. However, once a degree of trust is established this becomes a good basis for further exploration and development of therapeutic possibilities. But it should never be taken for granted!

2. A Serious Manner and a Gentle Touch

In the example of the noisy family in Chap. 4, I illustrated how joining in the light and jocular atmosphere in the waiting room was an important first step in creating a more focused and serious tone in subsequent sessions. The tip here is to watch and listen to one's own "internal conversation," that is, our in the moment internal reflections based on our sensorial responses to the mood we pick up from the family. In this initial meeting I felt that within the laughter and noise resided a wariness about coming to a family therapist and an awkwardness about the whole idea of therapy. I noticed looks of apprehension when I entered the waiting room to greet the family. It was at that point that one family member said, teasingly, that I looked like Billy Connolly the Scottish comedian. This allowed me to respond with a light, humorous manner that eased the initial noise of apprehension.

Adaptability is the key to all these "dance steps" and no two therapists will have the same range of responses.The overarching point is to focus on both initiating a connection with children and families and simultaneously being prepared to shift position as a conversation opens up.

Family members' prior experiences of therapists and other professionals may colour their initial perception of one's attempts to join them. Some therapists' default position is to offer a proximal, warm connection, whereas others are more measured in their initial move towards their clients. Neither position is problematic, but the skill is in manoeuvrability" one's capacity to be sure-footed yet able to move towards a mutually acknowledged relational trust, if only provisional.

For example, I have noticed that some men feel that a male therapist constitutes a challenge to their status within their family. This is usually accompanied by a scepticism about the idea of therapy as a useful activity in problem solving. Here the biggest mistakes I could make would be in becoming highly technical in my use of jargon, especially if I am lured into trying to assert my expertise in the face of scepticism or attempting to convince the person concerned of the credentials of my systemic approach.

Aside: Sometimes one needs to respond to the implicit message within the question stated. One very sceptical father in a family session asked within the first minute of meeting me: "What is your approach, how does it work and what do you do that is supposed to help?" The questions are legitimate and worthy of clarification. But the tone of the man's questions was aggressive, challenging and intended to intimidate. I needed to both allow myself some time to respond to the stated questions but more importantly to try to address his annoyance at having to attend the session at his wife's insistence.

I replied in a light tone, acknowledging the importance of his questions (approximate wording: "Good questions! We can certainly discuss how we can work and the aims of my approach. But first I'd like to hear your views on being invited to come to the session." This response shifted attention to the message within his words of sharp enquiry.

3. A Matter of Style and Timing: When to Wait and When to Intervene

When I was learning about the style and structure of the reflecting team as a useful method in family therapy (Andersen, 1990), it became accepted practice to offer reflections in a tentative, often "wondering," reverential tone of voice. Now while this quiet reflective style may be useful with certain families, it becomes a problem when teams behave as if this is the only way to offer reflections. Yet in family sessions, as I have described in this book, the style of the family and the style of the therapist need to have some degree of difference but also a measure of connection in manner and language to generate a joint direction in the therapy.

If a therapist's manner is seen by clients as overly gentle or too quiet, this can create problems in co-ordinating the relational practice that is needed.

When a family is in open conflict and needs a more interventive conductor of a therapy session, the too quiet therapist will be in trouble. The ability required here is to de-escalate noisy conflict and to somehow take charge and find ways to recalibrate the session. It requires an ability to intervene without insulting the clients. Sensitively worded interruptions by a therapist are sometimes necessary to allow other participants a voice in the proceedings. For example, one might say: *"Can we draw a halt for a minute here please? I need to pause for thought! It's so busy with so many voices can you let me just focus firstly on what you just said Mr J?"*

Or "Hold it please. Can we have 'one singer one song'? I need to pay attention to what you are all saying so can we just go back to what Mrs J just said?"

To interject and interrupt the flow of redundant interactions is part of a therapist's repertoire and can legitimately include robust challenges. These are not fuelled by anger or desperation but by a belief that the context of practice needs to be safe enough for all participants and structured enough for participants to feel their words will be respected.

Seconds Out!

I remember working with a teenage girl and her mother who came to a first therapy session ready for an almighty argument. Before I'd discussed how we would meet together, the daughter launched into a tirade of criticism against her mother. This led to raised voices and an all-out row. My co-therapist and I were taken aback. I tried to intervene (like a boxing referee?) but to no avail. The argument continued. Eventually I sat between the two combatants and said, "This is like being on one of those TV shows where everybody shouts at one another!!" This made a slight difference to the tone of the session and stopped the argument escalating further. We struggled to find common ground but avoided all-out warfare between them.

Sometimes addressing the pattern of interaction between feuding family members can help. For example: *"Is this how you do your arguments at home?"* or *"When you row like this, how does it usually end/become resolved?" or "Is this your usual way of sorting out problems?" or "Are there other ways to figure things out other than arguing?" or "When you row like this, what is not being said in all the noise of arguments?"*

In other words, the therapist tries to address the interactional pattern and the possible function of such heightened emotion and poses questions and fresh alternatives to try to create a more useful direction in the session. Arguments can be constructive and/or destructive, so it is important not to allow one's personal discomfort to automatically close down an argument because we are finding it uncomfortable.

The main aim is to focus on the meaning of dispute and argumentation in each unique encounter with a family. We need to be careful not to impose a prejudice that all argument and oppositional opinions are intrinsically destructive patterns of relating. The point is to check whether the argument is useful to the clients whilst keeping in mind one's concern to stop argumentation escalating into abusive behaviour.

To support and facilitate a person's expression of opinion and offer a useful response are part of a therapist's skills repertoire. Sensitivity to appreciate when to wait and savour the silence in a therapy session is part of the dance of intimacy already discussed in many of the case examples. A therapist must also decide when waiting and saying nothing is part of a redundant pattern in a family interview. Here the "dance" step required is more active, more interventive and more robust.

When Words Say Too Much

I have described already how important it is to judge when to speak in order to listen to our clients and when to listen in order to speak. For example, at times powerful feelings of sadness can tempt a therapist into speaking in order to stop sadness from dwelling too long in the atmosphere of a session. However, it is a fine judgement to decide whether a powerful expression of sadness or grief or guilt should be heard and acknowledged without trying to lighten the tone of a session. A therapist may sense that the silence accompanying sadness is reverential and worthy of respect. On other occasions the silence may be felt by a family member as oppressive, humiliating and exposing, and may call for words of sympathy or reassurance from a therapist rather than prolonging the silence. The therapist must pay attention to her embodied response, her observations and sympathetic presence with the child or family. It is important to listen to one's "hunches" as to how to respond to such experiences. At times I have asked my clients, "Shall we stay in silence for now?" Or I notice that I sigh as if in rhythm with the sadness expressed by my client. Perhaps the biggest mistake is to move too quickly to reassure or intrude on another person's feelings. We need to learn to wait without words until an invitation to speak arises. Such invitations are often sensed, and clients may offer cues in small movements of the body or facial expression as if signalling to a therapist to continue.

Therapy as an Improvisational Craft

I have illustrated elsewhere in the book the ways in which family therapists may include a range of physical movements in therapy sessions and how "getting out of the chair" is a necessary step to consider. It is apparent that a capacity for stillness and quiet reflection is also part of the therapist's repertoire. In all the steps outlined in this section there is one principle that connects all of them. It is the willingness and ability to be flexible in response to the unique offerings from our clients. This ability is a form of systemic improvisation: reading the context, judging how best to connect and support participants. Alongside supportive connection sits one's ability to challenge participants' ways of relating, thinking and experiencing one another. This emphasis on flexibility returns to the importance of improvisation in practice, a theme that weaves through the approach to practice I describe in this text.

In 2006 I was listening to the Reith lectures delivered by Daniel Barenboim and managed to capture his view on improvisation in music as "…the highest form of art … because when you see a score for the first time, and you don't know it, and you don't understand it, you have only a gut reaction to it. The first reaction is gut, instinct. … Then we take the music and we analyse it. And at that stage of the proceedings we have lost a lot of the freshness … we have forgotten the gut completely and we are only thinking. … But if we play like this we are not doing any art. We only get to this possible stage of making music the moment we have digested all that and we achieve a kind ***of conscious naivete which allows us to improvise it … at that moment as if it is on the spur of the moment***" (Barenboim, 2006, in Wilson, 2007).

If we replace the term "musical score" with "templates for practice" the analogy suggests that when we begin to learn about the theory, methods and techniques to employ as a systemic therapist, we lose our "gut instinct" the more we analyse. This is a necessary step in learning. It takes time to absorb ideas and new ways of practising. At a certain point we put our studies into practice. Here we learn to practise with *conscious naiveté* as if all is on the spur of the moment. To improvise in building creative bridges with children and families requires both the discipline of rigorous study and an ability to practise as if on the spur of the moment. It takes time! We do not play at being serious we are playfully serious.

This section has attempted to describe moment-to-moment complex interactions in family therapy that can only approximate the richness of any human encounter. However, attention to our attempts to create a fitting connection with each client is vital because these are the building blocks for co-creative practice.

Professor of Communication John Shotter (2016) warns that the absence of creative dialogue can lead "to fragmentation separation, disagreement, mistrust, alienation and even anger and non-cooperation" in matters of life. So, the fabric of effective human connection with children and families must be woven together in what Freire identifies as "a profound trust in people and their creative power."

In the next chapter I return in more detail to my practice philosophy, intending to invite your opinion and personal considerations about the ways you conduct yourself and the values you express in your meetings with others in your practice with children and families. In addition, I offer some retrospection on what I have tried to learn in my forty-five years involved in working, one way or another, with children and families. The door is always open to new possibilities.

References

Andersen, T. (Ed.). (1990). *The reflecting team*. Norton.

Fazzolari, B., (2022). bell hooks & Paulo Freire. A Critique of Transgressive Teaching & Critical Pedagogy. Tarija Sur. Printed in Great Britain by Amazon.

Freire, P. (1996). *Pedagogy of the oppressed*. Penguin.

Gawande, A. (2014). Reith lecture: The idea of wellbeing. *BBC Broadcast*, 20 December 2014.

Hoffman, L. (2002). *Family therapy: An intimate history*. W.W. Norton.

Shotter, J. (2016). *Speaking, actually: Towards a new fluid common-sense understanding of relational becomings*. Everything is Connected Press.
Stern, D. (2004). *The present moment in psychotherapy and everyday life*. W.W. Norton.
Wampold, B. E. (2001). *The great psychotherapy debate; models, methods, and findings*. Lawrence Erlbaum.
Wilson, J. (1998). *Child focused practice: A collaborative systemic approach*. Karnac.
Wilson, J. (2007). *The performance of practice: Enhancing the repertoire of therapy with children and families*. Karnac.
Wilson, J. (2011). On becoming a possibilist: Some influences from brief therapies. In *Context*, December.
Wilson, J. (2015). Family therapy as a process of humanisation: The contribution and creativity of dialogism. *Australian and New Zealand Journal of Family Therapy, 36*(1), 6–19.
Wilson, J. (2017). *Creativity in times of constraint: A practitioner's companion in mental health and social care*. Routledge.

7

Radical Systemic Humanism: Retrospection, and Towards a Philosophy of Practice

Hope is not the conviction that something will turn out well, but the certainty that something makes sense regardless of how it turns out.
—Havel (1991, p. 181)

A playfully serious orientation to practice with children and young people does not demand of a therapist exceptional skill but it does require an attitude of experimentation, rigorous thinking and a playful imagination. However, as the children's cases discussed here reveal, what matters most is the therapist's capacity to tap the resourcefulness and possibilities within the child and those important members of the child's network. I have also placed creative practices within a political context, one that takes account of factors that either restrict or promote co-creativity between colleagues as well as between therapist and clients. Without this wider reality being taken into account, the practitioner is left in something of a contextual vacuum, where all that matters is method, technique and closing an eye on the forces that operate to shape our social world and our therapeutic efforts. Practice is considered within this wider

J. Wilson, *Building Creative Therapeutic Relationships with Children and Young People*, Palgrave Texts in Counselling and Psychotherapy,
https://doi.org/10.1007/978-3-031-85706-5_7

macrocosm of a socio-political framework whilst also attending to the microcosm of particularities of a family therapy session (Wilson, 2013).

In recalling the children I have mentioned in these pages, I remind myself of the significance of small events leading the way to substantial changes. While we cannot predict outcomes, we can nevertheless engage in a process of hopeful and creative exploration that is therapeutic.

Small expressive movements like Yasmin's comforting of the toy tortoise or Jason's look of desperation that burst into life when he said "It's not me that needs the fucking therapy. It's her!" are the "invitations" from our young clients, and our job is to notice, accept and respond creatively to the invitations when they come.

Novelty and uncertainty in practice are necessary to entertain rather than fear. Amy joining me as co-chair to bring her family to therapy was a creative risk she was willing to take with me, and a mark of her courage in the face of her terminal illness. To improvise and spontaneously respond in practice does not mean leaving knowledge, research findings, protocols and formulations out in the cold. It emphasises the importance of the present moment in the therapeutic endeavour, and it reminds us not to think too far ahead or to rush to conclusions.

To take risks in practice we need to feel safe enough to improvise and respond without losing sight of our attempt to connect with our clients. The aim is to introduce a "not too unusual difference" into the dialogue (attributed to the late Tom Andersen).

The courage of the clients I've mentioned is an inspiration. If our young clients and their families are willing to take a risk in trusting us with their vulnerabilities and failures, we should similarly draw inspiration and continue to take responsible and well-considered risks to challenge and extend our ways of working therapeutically.

I began with the tragic events that led to Arthur's death to emphasise that creativity in child-focused practice is rooted in finding ways for a child's life to be protected and enhanced and for them to be given opportunities for their own creative possibilities to emerge. Yasmin and Jason, whose lives we have glimpsed, illustrate the possibilities that grow when you try to build creative bridges with your clients. Your young clients will have abilities to bring to bear on the problems they are facing and, while there are no miracle cures or magical answers, good practice and hopeful endeavours are more likely to occur when practitioners take creative risks and use their resources to expand therapeutic possibilities.

If therapy and psychosocial practices are to continue to develop, we need to be prepared to experiment, to take new steps in trying to improve on "what works" for children (Carr, 2000). Practice is a craft within a rigorous theoretical foundation informed by research. It is also a relational process rooted in connectionist, humanising values and situated within political and organisational structures. These political and organisational structures have a powerful influence on how services to children are provided and on the practitioners and therapists who work within these contexts.

Retrospection and the Bigger Picture

Building creative relationships with children and families is guided by an attitude of playful seriousness that is sustained by my experiences of working alongside creative colleagues. I invite you, dear reader, to consider the following retrospection on what really matters in your desire to remain creative and positive in your work as a therapist and systemically informed practitioner.

> ...to live well we must be able to imaginatively identify with other people and allow them to identify with us. Unkindness involves a failure of the imagination so acute that it threatens not just our happiness but our sanity: Caring for others ... is what makes us fully human. (Phillips & Taylor, 2009, p. 97)

I have emphasised in this book that building creative relationships relies on an attitude that questions practices that would limit and stultify creativity. This attitude is nurtured by contextual features that need to be in place for such rich critical thinking and practice to develop. Inspiration can come from any source but, importantly, such sources must be bolstered by a working environment that values the complexity of practice, the vulnerabilities of staff, and the recognition of good practice by peers and managers. This is a form of kindness: to care about clients and colleagues and care for us! Many family therapists acquire knowledge from theories, methods, techniques and approaches to practice, and all are vitally important, but at the heart of practice is an ability to bring a generosity of spirit into what we are doing. When tired and bereft of ideas, the rejuvenation of my practice depended on those colleagues who helped to keep my curiosity alive and my commitment well fuelled.

The foregoing examples emphasise that building creative relationships with children includes a focus on their significant network and may well involve friendships, extended family members and resourceful other professionals. The family therapist widens the field of vision to see more clearly whom to include in any therapy or network session.

Playing with variations on how to modify reflecting teams and the playful repositioning of therapists in the previous illustrations exemplify how systemic approaches can be enriched by repositioning our clients in more co-operative and co-creative directions. However, not all practice is possible from a connectionist orientation and, as I have emphasised, there is a need to be clear, to distinguish between a co-operative connection with clients as distinct from situations where statutory intervention and investigation is necessary. This should not stop the practitioner from holding firm to a belief in practice as a process of mutual humanisation even when called to intervene in situations where an adversarial context dominates the relationships with clients.

As a young social worker in Scotland, all reception into care actions was dealt with as a team approach. Colleagues making the enquiry about suspected abuse acted in co-ordination with team members who assisted in decision making and any practical arrangements. No one felt isolated with the sole responsibility to decide on action. Consultation was the key ingredient alongside time for reflection on actions taken. It was a communal effort. In such supportive networks, the parents of children who had been abused were less likely to be treated in a dehumanising manner. In the flurry of activity and heightened emotion, the team helped to focus the practice on finding appropriate actions without treating the parents in ways that objectified or dehumanised them. This is a difficult position to maintain, but my team colleagues helped me to hold onto humanising practices in the face of such painful experiences. Put starkly, observing such neglect and punishment of young children raises one's "hackles" and creates a desire to punish. It is an understandable reaction but not a useful response in one's attempt to provide a service that tries to maintain a sense of social justice. This is where we need the humanising influence of others to counter the "oppressor" inside. Freire argues that none of us are exempt from becoming the oppressor.

The Allure of the New and the Importance of Humility

My early family therapy training did not emphasise the importance of the therapist's embodied responses or emotions as a central consideration in practice. Instead, the dominant model of therapy I pursued was informed by strategic and early Milan Systemic approaches that emphasised interrupting communication patterns, treating the individual as more of a "black box" entwined in redundant patterns of interaction often requiring a paradoxical injunction to interrupt homeostatic patterns of communication. The language we used was full of cybernetic terms and therapists like me were fascinated by the allure of the cybernetic paradigm in therapy. These approaches offered a heady combination of systemic hypothesising and intellectual wizardry to create interventions that would impact directly on dysfunctional patterns of relationship. (Note the style of this pseudo-scientific language.) I eagerly subscribed to this exciting way of working. I mention this here because each of us will have a set of assumptions and biases that feel right when we work as a therapist. In this text I have argued that a therapy that is informed by systemic and related theories can provide a useful orientation to help children and families. I have clearly moved to entertain many different ideas about what works in systemic therapy and have emphasised co-creativity as a product of the inherent creativity in every person. We improvise all the time and draw on useful ideas from whichever source. I have not rejected strategic thinking or the formulations of the Milan approach. They can be extremely useful. But my view of systemic therapy as a process of mutual humanisation provides a congruence between what I tried to do as a therapist and what I believe to be an effective and ethical way of working. I have found a fit between my ideals as a human being and a way of meeting clients. However, I also know that we should never become complacent. Ideas change and therapeutic methods vary and evolve. The main ingredient is to continue to develop and explore new possibilities.

> Knowledge emerges only through invention and re-invention, through the restless, impatient continuing, hopeful inquiry human beings pursue in the world, and with each other. (Freire, 1996, p. 53)

I visited Michel De Montaigne's tower with my son a couple of years ago. I was drawn to visit the place where he retired from the world to write his famous essays in the sixteenth century when France was in the grip of political upheaval. I have always admired the essays for their exposure of human vulnerability and contradictions in entertaining life's uncertainties and paradoxes. One key dictum of Montaigne is "Que Je sais?" (What do I know?) (De Montaigne, 2004) This question sobers the mind from the intoxication of having definitive, unalterable views on any matter. It does not stop me from holding values or convictions about what could create a better therapy, a better society, a better life. But it does help me to pause and to open myself to other ideas, to allow for the fresh air of new perspectives, of debate and disagreement, so long as they contribute towards a richer, more creative endeavour as a therapist or teacher or becoming a better human being.

Radical Systemic Humanism: Towards a Philosophy of Systemic Practice

I have proposed elsewhere (Wilson, 2017) that systemic thinking and practice can be enriched by arguing for radical systemic humanism as a practice philosophy. I have interspersed the text with ideas based on Freire's radical humanism to illustrate my orientation. In this section I draw these together to address the overarching ideas informing radical systemic humanism as a philosophy of practice for you to consider.

This practice philosophy proposes that theories, methods, techniques and technologies of social practices should be placed in the service of mutual humanisation, recognising that "the pursuit of full humanity cannot be carried out in isolation or individualism, but only in fellowship and solidarity; therefore it cannot unfold in antagonistic relations between oppressor and oppressed. No one can be authentically human while he prevents others from being so" (Freire, 1996, p. 66). I have quoted Freire from time to time in the body of the text to emphasise the value of considering systemic therapy as an expression of mutual humanisation. Radical humanism is a philosophical orientation that provides coherence with my actions and beliefs as a therapist informed by systemic, collaborative, connectionist and dialogical approaches. The following section is intended to supplement the references to Freire in the body of the text and to reinforce the emphasis on co-creativity. I also include contributions from other writers whose ideas are congruent with this philosophy of practice.

On the Ideals of Mutual Humanisation and Creative Potential

> From the outset (the) effort of (the radical humanist) must coincide with those of the students to engage in critical thinking and the quest for mutual humanisation. ***His efforts must be imbued with a profound trust in people and their creative power.*** (Freire, 1996, p. 56)

This quote emphasises the co-creative predisposition of Freire's views on education. For the therapist, the same principle holds. It invites us to open ourselves to the view that our efforts to assist our clients are imbued with trust in the creative power of the people we meet. Clients in distress may feel their creativity has deserted them, and as mentioned earlier, the therapist needs to find ways to spark a creative opportunity. The emergence of fresh perspectives, joint action and a sense of empowerment are aims and outcomes of effective therapy and team consultations. Yet, this power is not always tapped in a family therapy session or in social practices, but it is a core value to hold because it provides an ideal worth striving towards and motivates practitioners towards co-creativity in their practices. The Possibilist therapist sees opportunities as to what can be achieved, and this attitude is cognisant of a belief in the latent creativity of the people we meet as patients or clients.

Creativity as an Invitation to Challenge the Status Quo

> Creativity is challenge—a sense that something is not right, leads us to creativity to challenge, to resist and to ask the question—'why is this so?.' We learn by questioning. How can you believe in something without questioning it? We get organised by a fear of offending the status quo. Creativity includes acts of dissidence. (Nawal El Saadawi personal communication Bristol 2015)

Acts of dissidence or disobedience are considered constructive.

Acts of dissidence in Saadawi's terms emphasises an activist and advocacy position in situations where the status quo crushes creativity or, worse, supports poor or dehumanising practices. But what form does this dissidence or disobedience take? Erich Fromm, social philosopher and psychoanalyst, proposes that

> Disobedience … is an act of reason and will. It is not primarily an attitude against something, but ***for*** something: for our capacity to see, to say what we see, and to refuse to say what we do not see. To do so we do not need to be aggressive … we need to have our eyes open, to be fully awake and willing to take responsibility to open the eyes of those who are in danger of perishing because they are half asleep. (Fromm, 1981, p. 24)

Both these writers, one a political activist and the other a social philosopher, propose action against unquestioning acceptance of a status quo that oppresses and confines a human being. Fromm suggests that awareness of such confined thinking is the first step to acting against oppressive practices. Freire's concept of magical thinking has already been addressed in Chap. 6 and corresponds to the call for the therapist to guard against becoming a victim of a circle of certainty. Instead, Fromm alerts us to remain vigilant to political forces pushing, as if from behind our backs, that would work against co-creativity in practice.

In our professional and personal lives, we are provoked to challenge "domestication," a naïve acceptance of a given set of circumstances, as if unalterable. The aim is to raise critical awareness and action to break free from such domesticated, blinkered thinking. For the therapist this raises the question of how to challenge professional and organisational conditions that would domesticate creativity or fail to act against dehumanising practices. Ken Robinson (2001), educationalist, describes this phenomenon as a contrast between aesthetic and anaesthetic educational systems and practices. He criticises certain formal processes of education as anaesthetic in their emphasis on standardisation and conformity, rooted in an industrial model of education within a structured hierarchically organised system. Aesthetic education, on the other hand, is based upon an organic growth metaphor that is experimentalist, less hierarchical, and encourages diversity in thinking and practice. This aesthetic orientation in education sits comfortably with the playfully serious orientation of family therapy described here. It does not mean that all structures, protocols and models of practice are intrinsically anaesthetic. Rather, an aesthetic, organic orientation emphasises the need to modify, improvise and particularise each standard practice to fit the unique circumstances of each family in therapy. To keep the connection with clients a mutually humanising process the therapist avoids a technocratic approach. Co-operation is the key aim and co-creativity the main focus for the therapist. The model of practice is in the service of creative human connection, not the other way around.

The Importance of Joint Action Against Dehumanisation

As a systemic family therapist, joint action is a preferred position when meeting children and their families in therapy. Though, as mentioned earlier, it is not always possible to meet with all the significant people in a child's life, this is a preferred premise towards practice. Freire's philosophy supports this emphasis on relational and communal ways of promoting full humanity that cannot be carried out in individualism but only in solidarity. Freire argues that the opposite process, dehumanisation, is expressed in self-subjugation, cruelty, acts of injustice and exploitation. These dehumanising processes may occur in social care or mental health services where abuse of patients has taken place, or where social causes of personal distress are defined as expressions of individual pathology and personal weakness. Dehumanisation strangles dialogue. Therapy that opposes dehumanisation is based on generative dialogical processes and a relationally creative endeavour aimed at countering oppressive practices. This approach is not confined only to the specifics of a family therapy session. The barrier between the therapy room and the world outside is made transparent. Therapy is a micro political activity within a macro political system. We are therefore obliged to engage critically with the wider systems that impact practice. I have already addressed the benefits of upholding joint teamwork, opening practices to engage others, developing an attitude of engagement with different approaches, sharing of support and vulnerability between practitioners, and action against forces that inhibit humanising practice. These are crucial features in sustaining co-creativity with the children, young people and families we meet.

On Improvisation, Spontaneity and Practice

I have also placed an emphasis on the micro relational features in therapy that emphasise the range of responses that constitute a form of relational "dance" between participants. This focuses our attention on the sensorial aspects of building creative relationships with clients and requires informed spontaneity based on critical reflection ***and*** scope for improvisation and the spontaneous gesture. Improvisation is not an "anything goes" attitude. It is bound by the obligation of the practitioner to uphold practice as a mutually humanising process. Improvisations associated with spontaneity are acts that are embedded in a position of professional care, reflection-in-action. The judgement of the therapist informs what improvisational moves may engender curiosity from the family members.

The storytelling, the playing with family members in reflecting teams, role plays and other "in the moment" improvisations attempt to create new perspectives that free up new directions in therapy.

Improvisation in this sense is not an exceptional event in any communication. Spontaneous actions and improvisations are better understood as stemming from a prior experience and learning about "what works." To improvise, as in playing a musical instrument, requires practice, study, learning about music theory, developing the facility to hit the correct notes at the right time and so on. As with the earlier quote by Barenboim, we can see parallels whereby the unexpected creative gesture is not completely "out of the blue" but is informed by all our earlier experience and trial-and-error learning.

> We are all improvisers, continually improvising within the practices that we develop in our relationships with the world. We are improvisers every day, without realising it; most of the time we are unaware of the power of this generative process, while giving improvised and unexpected answers to events. We are all improvisers, even though we do not often acknowledge, even refusing it, relegating improvisation to the realm of crude spontaneism and evanescent episodes with neither stability, nor deep structural anchoring in consciousness and expertise.

End Note and a Meditation

Creativity in practice can never be divorced from the structural features that constrain or enhance possibilities to do a good job. Over my years in practice, I have benefitted from colleagues who had a similar commitment to do a good job, sometimes in conditions of high stress and work overload. Their encouragement sustained me. In all the demands of our practice there was time for teasing, humour, social events and celebrations, Friday night drinks "down the pub" (on occasion) and having a laugh. Without this matrix of benevolent irreverence, I think teamwork would have been less colourful, less warm and less caring. To become more playfully serious, we also benefit from the enrichment that comes from life outside our professional domains. What inspires you in life?

What do you value that keeps you keeping on? These dimensions of life matter in helping us all to be replenished by our own psychosocial resources.

I began this book by commenting that it was an opportunity to cut to the core of ideas that have charged and recharged my investment in systemic therapy since 1978. I return each time to the basic ideas of humility going hand in hand with expertise, professional distance, with appropriate emotional closeness, playfulness, with serious intent and rigour, respect for received wisdom and irreverence to challenge pomposity. One colleague described the position of a family therapist as someone who resides on the borderlands of ideas. To continue to develop as therapists and build better bridges with children we need to be able to cross over into fresh territory and refuse the temptation to remain still and cease exploration. To build creative relationships, whether in family therapy practice or in our lives beyond the professional domain, we can be at home on the borderlands, remaining open to invitations towards creative possibilities with those we meet.

With apologies to the poet John Donne, I have replaced "Man" with "Child" and "Mankind" with "Humankind" in the following famous quote from Meditation 17. It is a tribute to young Arthur Labinjo-Hughes.

> *No child is an island, entire of itself; every child is a piece of the continent, a part of the main; if a clod be washed away by the sea, Europe is the less, as well as if a promontory were, as well as if a manor of thy friend's or of thine own were; any child's death diminishes me, because I am involved in human kind, and therefore never send to know for whom the bell tolls; it tolls for thee.*

Neither is the practitioner an island.

References

Carr, A. (2000). *What works with children and adolescents?* Brunner-Routledge.
De Montaigne, M. (2004). *The essays: A selection.* Penguin.
Freire, P. (1996). *Pedagogy of the oppressed.* Penguin.

Fromm, E. (1981). *On disobedience. Why freedom means saying "no" to power.* Harper Perennial.
Phillips, A., & Taylor, B. (2009). *On Kindness.* London. Penguin.
Robinson, K. (2001). *Out of our minds: Learning to be creative.* Capstone.
Wilson, J. (2013). A social relational critique of the biomedical definition and treatment of ADHD: Ethical, practical and political implications. *Journal of Family Therapy, 36*, 6–19.
Wilson, J. (2017). *Creativity in times of constraint: A practitioner's companion in mental health and social care.* Routledge.

References

Andersen, T. (Ed.). (1990). *The reflecting team*. Norton.
Brady, G. (2005). ADHD, diagnosis, and identity. In C. Newnes & N. Radcliffe (Eds.), *Making and breaking children's lives*. PCCS Books.
Carr, A. (2000). *What works with children and adolescents?* Brunner-Routledge.
Cecchin, G. (1987). Hypothesising circularity and neutrality revisited: An invitation to curiosity. *Family Process, 26*, 405–413.
Cecchin, G., Lane, G., & Ray, W. (1992). *Irreverence: A strategy for therapists' survival*. Karnac Books.
Cecchin, G., Lane, G., & Ray, W. (1994). *The cybernetics of prejudices in the practice of psychotherapy*. Karnac.
Cole, E., John-Steiner,V., Scribner, S., & Souberman, E. (Eds). (1978) L. S. Vygotsky: Mind In Society; Development of Higher Psychological Processes. Cambridge: Harvard University Press.
Coleman, S. (Ed.). (1985). *Failures in family therapy*. Guilford Press.
Dallos, R., & Draper, R. (2010). *An introduction to family therapy: Systemic theory and practice*. Open University Press.
De Montaigne, M. (2004). *The essays: A selection*. Penguin.
Donaldson, M. (1978). *Children's Minds*. London: Fontana.
Donne, J. (n.d.). Meditation 17. In H. Alford (Ed.), *The works of John Donne, vol 3* (pp. 574–575). J.W. Parker.

J. Wilson, *Building Creative Therapeutic Relationships with Children and Young People*, Palgrave Texts in Counselling and Psychotherapy,
https://doi.org/10.1007/978-3-031-85706-5

Fazzolari, B., (2022). bell hooks & Paulo Freire. A Critique of Transgressive Teaching & Critical Pedagogy. Tarija Sur. Printed in Great Britain by Amazon.

Fisch, R., Weakland, J., & Segal, L. (1982). *The tactics of change: Doing therapy briefly*. Jossey-Bass.

Freire, P. (1996). *Pedagogy of the oppressed*. Penguin.

Freire, P. (1998). *Pedagogy of freedom*. Rowman & Littlefield.

Fromm, E. (1981). *On disobedience. Why freedom means saying "no" to power*. Harper Perennial.

Gawande, A. (2014). Reith lecture: The idea of wellbeing. *BBC Broadcast*, 20 December 2014.

Gergen, K. J. (2009). *Relational being: Beyond self and community*. Oxford University Press.

Grabbe, M. (2001). Kooperationmit Kindernin Therapieund Beratung. In A. von Schlippe, G. Losche, & C. Hawellek (Eds.), *FruhkindlicheLebenswelten und Erziehungsberatung. DieChancendesAnfangs* (pp. 220–242). Votum.

Havel, V. (1991). *Disturbing the peace*. Vintage.

Heimann, C. (2009). Guardian guide to performance, 9 May. *Guardian News and Media*.

Hoffman, L. (2002). *Family therapy: An intimate history*. W.W. Norton.

Jakob, P. (2022). *Dem Trauma Widerstand Leisten: Neue Autoritat als familientherapeutischer und traumapadagogischer Ansatz*. Vandenhoeck & Ruprecht.

Koestler, A. (1964). *The act of creation*. Arkana.

Mason, B. (1993). Towards positions of safe uncertainty. *Human Systems, 4*, 189–200.

McCarthy, I. C., & Byrne, N. O. (1988). Mis-taken love: Conversations on the problem of incest in an Irish context. *Family Process, 27*, 181–199.

Miller, S., & Hubble, M. (2011). The road to mastery. *Psychotherapy Networker, 35*(3), 22–31, 60.

Murray, J. (2021). Arthur Labinjo-Hughes: Timeline of events that ended in his murder. *Guardian Newspaper*.

Palazzoli, M., Boscolo, L., Cecchin, G., & Prata, G. (1978). *Paradox and counter-paradox*. Jason Aronson.

Palazzoli, M., Boscolo, L., Cecchin, G., & Prata, G. (1980a). Hypothesising, circularity, neutrality: Three guidelines for the conductor of the interview. *Family Process, 19*(1), 3–11.

Palazzoli, M., Boscolo, L., Cecchin, G., & Prata, G. (1980b). The problem of the referring person. *Journal of Marital and Family Therapy, 6*, 3–9.

Phillips, A., & Taylor, B. (2009). *On Kindness*. London. Penguin.

Robinson, K. (2001). *Out of our minds: Learning to be creative*. Capstone.

Santi, M. (Ed.). (2010). *Improvisation: Between technique and spontaneity*. Cambridge Scholars Publishing.

Schon, D. A. (1986). *The reflective practitioner: How professionals think in action*. Basic Books.

Seikkula, J., & Arnkil, T. E. (2014). *Open dialogues and anticipations: Respecting otherness in the personal moment*. National Institute for Health and Welfare.

Shepherd, R., Johns, J., & Taylor Robinson, H (eds) (1996). D. W. Winnicott: Thinking About Children. London. Karnac.

Shotter, J. (2016). *Speaking, actually: Towards a new fluid common-sense understanding of relational becomings*. Everything is Connected Press.

Stern, D. (2004). *The present moment in psychotherapy and everyday life*. W.W. Norton.

Sternberg, R. J. (Ed.). (2010). *Handbook of creativity*. Cambridge University Press.

Stith, S., Rosens, K. H., McCollum, E. E., Coleman, J. U., & Herman, S. A. (1996). *Journal of Marital and Family Therapy, 22*, 69–86.

Timimi, S. (2007). *Mis-understanding ADHD: The complete guide for parents to alternatives to drugs*. Author House.

Timimi, S. (2009). *Straight talking introduction to children's mental health problems*. PCCS Books.

Timimi, S., & Leo, J. (Eds.). (2009). *Rethinking ADHD: From brain to culture*. Palgrave Macmillan.

Wampold, B. E. (2001). *The great psychotherapy debate; models, methods, and findings*. Lawrence Erlbaum.

Wampold, B. E. (2015). How important are the common factors in psychotherapy? An update. *World Psychiatry, 14*(3), 270–277.

Watzlawick, P., Weakland, J., & Fisch, R. (1974). *Change: Principles of problem formation and problem resolution*. W.W. Norton & Co.

White, M. (2011). *Narrative practice: Continuing the conversation* (D. Denborough, Ed.). Norton.

White, M., & Epston, M. (1990). *Narrative means to therapeutic ends*. W.W. Norton.

Wilson, J. (1998). *Child focused practice: A collaborative systemic approach*. Karnac.

Wilson, J. (2003). *Kindorientierte Therapie: Ein systemisch-kooperativer Ansatz*. Carl-Auer-Systeme Verlag.

Wilson, J. (2006). *Woran erkennt man,ob ein Goldfisch weint? Wie man Bilder fur therapeutische Geschichten mit Kinder findet*. In Systhema vol 1 Jahrgang - Seite 5–13.

Wilson, J. (2007). *The performance of practice: Enhancing the repertoire of therapy with children and families*. Karnac.

Wilson, J. (2011). On becoming a possibilist: Some influences from brief therapies. In *Context*, December.

Wilson, J. (2013). A social relational critique of the biomedical definition and treatment of ADHD: Ethical, practical and political implications. *Journal of Family Therapy, 36*, 6–19.

Wilson, J. (2015). Family therapy as a process of humanisation: The contribution and creativity of dialogism. *Australian and New Zealand Journal of Family Therapy, 36*(1), 6–19.

Wilson, J. (2016). Engaging children and young people; A theatre of possibilities. In *Narrative therapies with children and their families* (A practitioner's guide to concepts and approaches) (2nd ed., pp. 91–111). Routledge.

Wilson, J. (2017). *Creativity in times of constraint: A practitioner's companion in mental health and social care*. Routledge.

Wilson, J. (2021). Boxed in?: Commentary on widening the screen: Playful responses to challenges in online therapy with children and families. *Journal of Family Therapy, 43*(2), 346–350.

Index

J. Wilson, *Building Creative Therapeutic Relationships with Children and Young People*, Palgrave Texts in Counselling and Psychotherapy,
https://doi.org/10.1007/978-3-031-85706-5